My iMovie®

Craig James Johnston
Cheryl Brumbaugh-Duncan

800 East 96th Street,
Indianapolis, Indiana 46240 USA

My iMovie®

Copyright © 2014 by Pearson Education

ISBN-13: 978-0-7897-4995-6
ISBN-10: 0-7897-4995-5

Library of Congress Control Number: 2014930245

Printed in the United States of America

First Printing: March 2014

Trademarks

All terms mentioned in this book that are known to be trademarks or service marks have been appropriately capitalized. Que Publishing cannot attest to the accuracy of this information. Use of a term in this book should not be regarded as affecting the validity of any trademark or service mark.

Warning and Disclaimer

Every effort has been made to make this book as complete and as accurate as possible, but no warranty or fitness is implied. The information provided is on an "as is" basis. The author and the publisher shall have neither liability nor responsibility to any person or entity with respect to any loss or damages arising from the information contained in this book or from the use of the programs accompanying it.

Special Sales

For information about buying this title in bulk quantities, or for special sales opportunities (which may include electronic versions; custom cover designs; and content particular to your business, training goals, marketing focus, or branding interests), please contact our corporate sales department at corpsales@pearsoned.com or (800) 382-3419.

For government sales inquiries, please contact governmentsales@pearsoned.com.

For questions about sales outside the U.S., please contact international@pearsoned.com.

Editor-in-Chief
Greg Wiegand

Senior Acquisitions Editor
Laura Norman

Development Editor
Charlotte Kughen

Managing Editor
Kristy Hart

Senior Project Editor
Lori Lyons

Copy Editor
Karen Annett

Indexer
Lisa Stumpf

Proofreader
Dan Knott

Technical Editor
Greg Kettell

Editorial Assistant
Cindy Teeters

Cover Designer
Mark Shirar

Compositor
Bronkella Publishing

Manufacturing Buyer
Dan Uhrig

Contents at a Glance

Table of Contents

About the Authors

Craig James Johnston has been involved with technology since his high school days at Glenwood High in Durban, South Africa, when his school was given some Apple][Europluses. From that moment, technology captivated him and he has owned, supported, evangelized, and written about it.

Craig has been involved in designing and supporting large-scale enterprise networks with integrated email and directory services since 1989. He has held many different IT-related positions in his career ranging from sales support engineer to mobile architect for a 40,000-smartphone infrastructure at a large bank.

In addition to designing and supporting mobile computing environments, Craig cohosts the CrackBerry.com podcast as well as guest hosting on other podcasts, including iPhone and iPad Live podcasts. You can see Craig's previously published work in his book *Professional BlackBerry*, and many books in the *My* series, including books covering BlackBerry, Palm, Nexus, HTC, DROID, and Samsung devices.

Craig also enjoys high-horsepower, high-speed vehicles and tries very hard to keep to the speed limit while driving them.

Originally from Durban, South Africa, Craig has lived in the United Kingdom, the San Francisco Bay Area, and New Jersey, where he now lives with his wife, Karen, and a couple of cats.

Craig would love to hear from you. Feel free to contact Craig about your experiences with *My iMovie* at http://www.CraigsBooks.info.

All comments, suggestions, and feedback are welcome, including positive and negative.

Cheryl Brumbaugh-Duncan is committed to education and technology. For more than 15 years Cheryl has run her own company, Virtually Global Communications - VGC, a Web design and development company with a focus in education. Armed with a Master's degree in Education, as well as being an expert in web design and development, she has been developing cutting-edge websites and mobile Internet applications, and teaching individuals and companies about computers, technology, and web design and development.

Combining web technologies and education strategies, Cheryl has developed and authored books, instructor-led training curriculum, and online education courses for clientele that include QWEST, Que, Alpha Publishing, New Riders Publishing, ADIC, Dell, Virtual Training Company–VTC, and Sun Microsystems.

Cheryl has been an avid Apple Computer enthusiast for years, ever since Apple captured the education market back in the 1980s. From that time until today, she has used Apple products for her work and personal use. She has authored and taught training classes on Apple products and has used the Apple iLife suite of software since it was introduced—this includes the iMovie software product.

Cheryl currently teaches college classes in web development and design. Her commitment to the combination of education, technology, and various delivery methods for communicating information keeps her very busy in this ever-changing world. Please visit her website at www.virtuallyglobal.com to learn more about Cheryl and her company Virtually Global Communications.

Dedication

"Human beings, who are almost unique in having the ability to learn from the experience of others, are also remarkable for their apparent disinclination to do so."
—*Douglas Adams*

I would like to dedicate this book to my Mom & Dad—my guiding stars!

Acknowledgments

Many thanks go to my agent, Carole Jelen of Waterside Productions, for her many years of service. I look forward to more projects and opportunities with you and Waterside Productions, Inc.

A big thank you to Craig James Johnston, my coauthor, for all his great writing, insight, ideas, and support throughout the book's development.

I also want to thank Laura Norman, Todd Brakke, Lori Lyons, and Greg Kettell, as well as all the other editors and designers of Que, for all their dedicated work, keen eyes, and helpful comments and suggestions. This book is much better due to everyone's efforts!

Thank you to Apple Computer for iMovie v10 and all their other products and software—they truly are innovators and leaders in today's fast-paced, technology-driven world.

I also want to thank my husband, David Duncan, for allowing the use of his African safari movies and photos for all the images and figures in this book. And finally, I cannot forget my beautiful daughter, Tasmin: thank you for being you!

—Cheryl

We Want to Hear from You!

As the reader of this book, *you* are our most important critic and commentator. We value your opinion and want to know what we're doing right, what we could do better, what areas you'd like to see us publish in, and any other words of wisdom you're willing to pass our way.

We welcome your comments. You can email or write to let us know what you did or didn't like about this book—as well as what we can do to make our books better.

Please note that we cannot help you with technical problems related to the topic of this book.

When you write, please be sure to include this book's title and author as well as your name and email address. We will carefully review your comments and share them with the author and editors who worked on the book.

Email: feedback@quepublishing.com

Mail: Que Publishing
         ATTN: Reader Feedback
         800 East 96th Street
         Indianapolis, IN 46240 USA

Reader Services

Visit our website and register this book at quepublishing.com/register for convenient access to any updates, downloads, or errata that might be available for this book.

Movie timeline

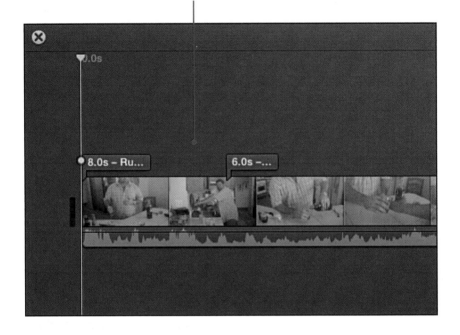

In this chapter, you become familiar with the iMovie screen layout, what each part of the screen does or is for, and some general iMovie concepts and terminology. Topics include the following:

→ Becoming familiar with the iMovie layout
→ Examining the project screen layout

Getting to Know iMovie General Concepts

Before you start using iMovie, you should become familiar with the way iMovie looks on your screen, what the different parts of the screen are, and some general terms that are used by iMovie.

iMovie Layout

Becoming familiar with the way that iMovie divides up the screen will allow you to navigate it with ease.

Libraries

On the left of the screen, in the left pane are the libraries. Anything you click on in the Libraries view is displayed in the top-middle pane in iMovie.

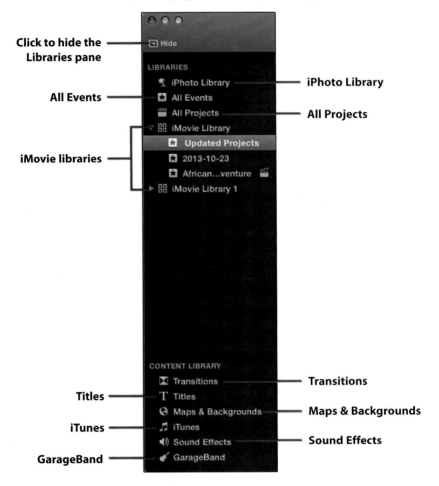

- **iPhoto Library**—When you click on iPhoto Library, you see all photos in your iPhoto Library. You can then search for, select, and drag photos into your movie timeline. Learn more about adding iPhoto images in Chapter 3, "Creating a New Movie Project."

- **All Events**—When you click All Events, you see all iMovie events (which are holder videos you have imported) in all iMovie libraries that you have chosen. You can find video footage in the events to drag to your movie timeline. Learn more about events in Chapter 2, "Importing and Organizing Video, Events, and Movie Clips."

- **All Projects**—When you click All Projects, you see all iMovie projects in all iMovie libraries that you have chosen. You can then double-click a project to make changes to it. Learn more about projects in Chapter 3.

- **iMovie Library**—iMovie libraries contain events and projects. You may have selected more than one iMovie Library. Expanding an iMovie Library enables you to see only events and projects in that library.

Content Library

The Content Library is only visible when you are editing an iMovie project. Anything you click in the Content Library is displayed in the top-middle pane in iMovie.

- **Transitions**—While editing an iMovie project, you can insert transitions between clips by finding them in the Transitions list and dragging them into your movie timeline. Learn more about transitions in Chapter 3.

- **Titles**—While editing an iMovie project, you can insert titles between clips or over clips by finding them in the Titles list and dragging them into your movie timeline. Learn more about titles in Chapter 5, "Adding Special Effects and Titles Clips."

- **Maps & Backgrounds**—While editing an iMovie project, you can insert maps and backgrounds between clips or over clips by finding them in the Maps & Backgrounds list and dragging them into your movie timeline. Read more about using maps in Chapter 5.

- **iTunes**—While editing an iMovie project, you can insert music from your iTunes library by finding it and dragging it into your movie timeline. Read more about adding music from your iTunes library in Chapter 6, "Adding and Editing Voiceovers, Music, and Sound Effects."

- **Sound Effects**—While editing an iMovie project, you can insert sound effects by finding them and dragging them into your movie timeline. Sound effects are also covered in Chapter 6.

- **GarageBand**—While editing an iMovie project, you can insert music or other audio from your GarageBand library by finding them and dragging them into your movie timeline. Working with audio from GarageBand is covered in Chapter 6.

Movie Timeline

When you create an iMovie project, the movie's timeline is shown in the Timeline view.

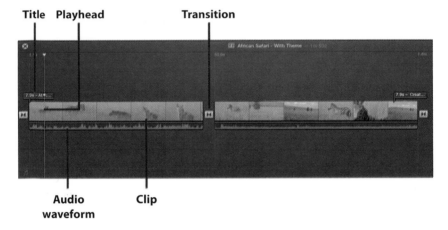

- **Title**—This shows where you have titles in your movie. Double-click a title to edit it.

- **Clip**—A clip is a part of your original video footage that you have used in your movie.

- **Transition**—This shows where you have used a transition between two clips. Double-click the transition to edit it.

- **Audio waveform**—This shows a visual representation of the audio that is associated with the clips in your movie.

- **Playhead**—The playhead indicates what part of your movie you are viewing in the Viewer pane. Click anywhere in your movie to make the playhead jump to that location. Press the spacebar to start playing your movie from the playhead. Press the spacebar again to stop playing the movie.

Viewer

The Viewer pane, which is on the top right of the screen, shows your movie when you are playing it, but also doubles as the area where you make all of your edits.

Viewer

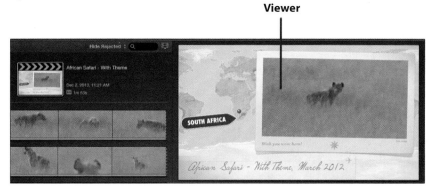

Browser

The Browser window allows you to browse content that you select in the Libraries list. This would be your raw video footage or a list of projects or events. In this example, we are browsing the transitions.

Browser

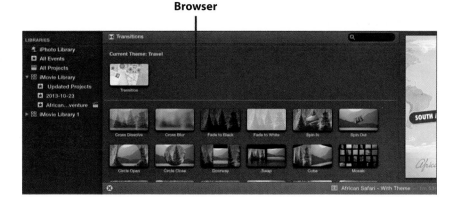

Theater

After you have finished creating your movie, you can save it to the iMovie Theater. Once there, you can easily access it in iMovie, or if you have allowed your theater to synchronize with your iCloud account, you can access the movies on any Apple device (including Apple TV) that is connected to that iCloud account.

Theater

Toolbar

The iMovie toolbar allows you quick access to commonly used functions.

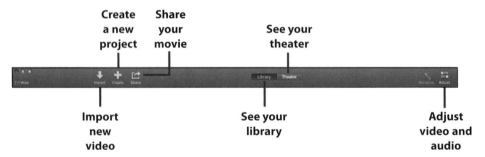

- **Create a new project**—Click here to create a new iMovie project. You will be able to choose whether your project uses a theme, and after it has been created, you will be able to drag movie clips into it.

- **Import new video**—Click here to import new video into iMovie so that you can use it in your movies. The video can come from memory cards or from your Mac's hard disk. You can also use cameras connected to your Mac (including the FaceTime camera) to import video in real time.

- **Share your movie**—Click here to share your movie project with others. iMovie offers many different ways to share your movie.

- **See your library**—Click to see your iMovie Library. This is the default view in iMovie and enables you to work on your movie projects.

- **See your theater**—Click to see your iMovie Theater, which contains all completed movies that you have chosen to import.

- **Adjust video and audio**—When you select all or part of a clip, you can use the Adjust menu to make changes not only to the look of the clip, but also to the way it sounds.

Libraries
list   Sidebar   Menu
bar   Event
Browser   Toolbar   Viewer

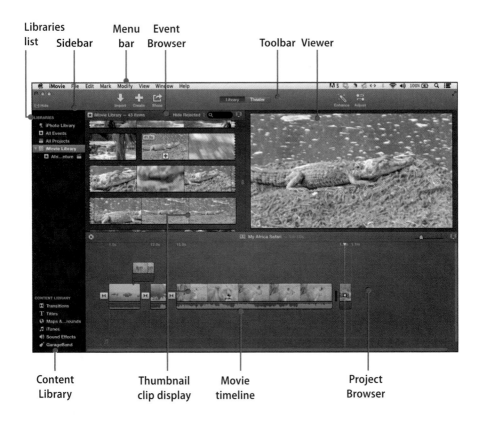

Content
Library   Thumbnail
clip display   Movie
timeline   Project
Browser

In this chapter, you learn about customizing the iMovie workspace and changing default preferences and settings. You also find out how to switch the location of the Project Browser and Event Browser as well as how to modify the size of other elements of the workspace and clip thumbnails. Topics include the following:

1

→ Rearranging and customizing the iMovie workspace
→ Switching Project Browser and Event Browser location
→ Modifying thumbnail clips
→ Wrapping a movie timeline
→ Customizing iMovie preferences
→ Changing default movie preferences

Customizing iMovie Settings and Preferences

When you first open iMovie, you see the default workspace. iMovie automatically sets default preferences that control functionality and settings of iMovie as well as any new movie project. You can modify these preferences and settings and also modify the display of the iMovie workspace.

The workspace is made up of the sidebar, Event Browser, Project Browser, and Viewer. The sidebar contains the Libraries list and the Content Library. The Event Browser is also referred to as the Browser because it can display projects, events, clips, photos, and sound files. The Project Browser contains the movie timeline. Both the Browser and movie timeline display thumbnail images of clips that are set to a default display size. You can modify the size and location of these workspace elements and modify the display of the thumbnail clips.

iMovie Workspace and the Project Browser

When you first install iMovie and you haven't opened a new project yet, the iMovie workspace displays just the sidebar, Event Browser, and Viewer. This is the iMovie default workspace layout.

When you create your first project (see Chapter 3) or open a project that you updated from an older version of iMovie (see Chapter 2), the workspace changes and the Project Browser displays at the bottom of the workspace with the Event Browser and Viewer above the Project Browser. You can close the Project Browser at any time by clicking the Close button, and the workspace reverts to the iMovie default layout.

Switching the Project and Event Browsers

You can modify and adjust the layout of the iMovie workspace. Say you need more space for displaying events, movie clips, and photos to add to your movie project. You can switch the position of the Project and Event Browsers.

1. Choose Window, Swap Project and Event.

2. The Project Browser and the Event Browser swap locations in the workspace.

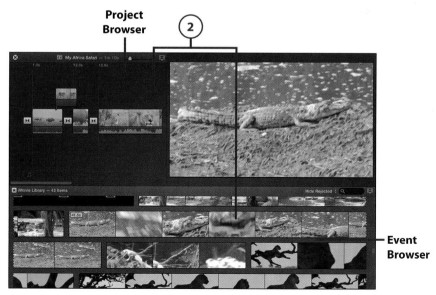

Project Browser

Event Browser

Reverting to the Default iMovie Workspace

If you have adjusted and modified the iMovie workspace, you can quickly reset the workspace to the default layout by choosing Window, Revert to Original Layout.

Reset the workspace to the default

Resizing the Sidebar, Viewer, Event Browser, and Project Browser

You can also adjust the size of the iMovie sidebar, Event Browser, Viewer, and Project Browser. When you increase the size of any of these, the other iMovie workspace elements resize according to the space available.

1. Position your cursor on the horizontal border between the Project Browser and the Viewer/Event Browser. When the mouse becomes the double-headed arrow tool, click and drag the border up or down to resize the Project Browser. The Event Browser and the Viewer resize according to the space available.

2. Position your cursor on the vertical border to the right of the iMovie sidebar and either the Event Browser or the Project Browser, respectively. When the mouse becomes the double-headed arrow tool, click and drag left or right to resize the sidebar. The Event Browser, Viewer, and the Project Browser resize in relation to the space available.

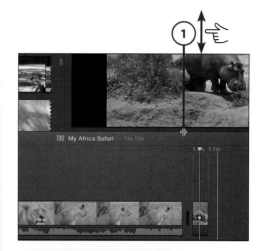

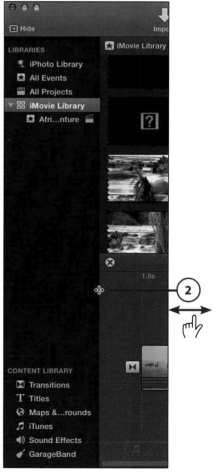

Hiding the iMovie Sidebar

The iMovie sidebar contains the Libraries list and the Content Library. After you have your movie laid out, you might not need to have this sidebar displayed. You can hide the sidebar to give you more room to work on your movie.

1. Click the Hide button to hide the Libraries sidebar. The button's label changes to Show after you click it.

2. Click the Show button to show the iMovie sidebar again.

Changing the Display of Project and Event Browser Content

You can change how things look in the Event Browser and Project Browser, such as the appearance of movie clips and the display of the timeline, as well as other default settings for applying Zoom to movie clips and the display of audio waveforms for audio tracks. You can have the timeline wrap in its display in the Project Browser, and increase or decrease the display of thumbnail images of the movie clips in both the Event and Project Browsers.

Wrap the Movie Timeline

By default, the movie timeline is displayed in one row that extends to the right until the movie ends. Often, movie projects are developed in a very long timeline. To see all the timeline, scroll right and left in the Project Browser by dragging the horizontal scrollbar. You can also make the movie timeline wrap in the Project Browser pane so that you can see more of it at a glance.

1. Select View, Wrapping Timeline.

2. The timeline wraps in the available width of the Project Browser. If your timeline extends farther down than what is displayed in the Project Browser, click and drag the vertical scrollbar.

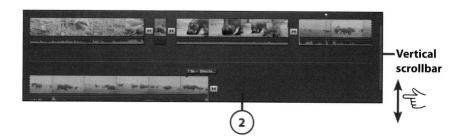

Vertical scrollbar

Adjust a Clip Thumbnail in the Event Browser

The Event Browser has a title bar at the top that includes the Adjust Thumbnail Appearance option. This option lets you adjust the size of the thumbnail image of each movie clip. You can increase the size of the thumbnail so you can focus on selecting the exact footage of the clip that you need for your movie.

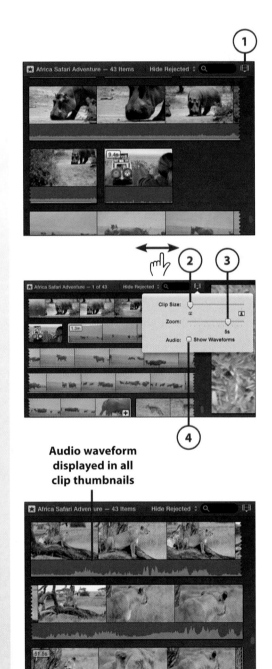

1. Click the Adjust Thumbnail Appearance option.

2. Adjust the Clip Size slider to decrease or increase the size of the thumbnail by clicking and dragging the slider left or right.

3. Decrease or increase the Zoom duration for the footage displayed in the clip thumbnail by dragging the Zoom slider left or right.

Zoom Feature of a Movie Clip

You can set the amount of footage that is shown in each clip thumbnail by adjusting the Zoom duration. Dragging the Zoom slider to the right increases the duration of the clip footage to display more video footage in the clip thumbnail, and dragging to the left decreases the duration of the zoom. The default setting is 5 seconds. This lets you skim more or less footage in the thumbnail display.

Audio waveform displayed in all clip thumbnails

4. Turn on the display of the audio track waveform in the clip by selecting the Show Waveforms check box. You can turn this off by deselecting this check box.

Adjust the Clip Thumbnail in the Project Browser

The Project Browser also has an Adjust Thumbnail Appearance option that works pretty much the same as the option in the Event Browser, although it has fewer options to configure. Use this option to adjust the size of the thumbnail image of each movie clip in the movie timeline. You can also use the Zoom In or Out on Clips slider for quick access to adjust the movie clip thumbnail size display in the timeline.

1. Click the Adjust Thumbnail Appearance option in the Project Browser.

2. Click and drag the Clip Size slider left or right to decrease or increase the clip thumbnail size.

3. Turn off the default display of audio track waveforms by removing the check mark from the Show Waveforms check box. Click the check box again to display the audio track waveforms.

4. Click and drag the Zoom slider to increase the amount of footage displayed in clip thumbnails.

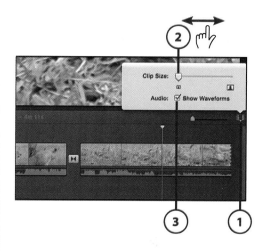

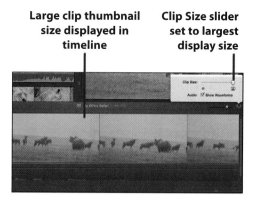

Large clip thumbnail size displayed in timeline

Clip Size slider set to largest display size

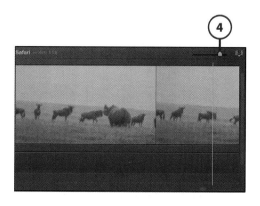

Showing Event Clips by Separate Days

The Event Browser can also display clips by the day it was recorded. To do this, select View, Show Separate Days in Events. You can also right-click anywhere in a blank area of the Browser and choose Show Separate Days in Events from the menu.

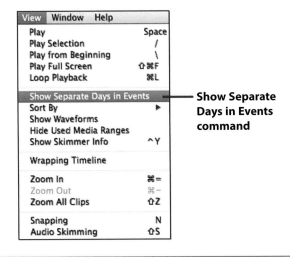

Show Separate Days in Events command

Setting iMovie Preferences

When you install iMovie, it's set up with default preferences that control whether slow motion is automatically added to any imported clips and if iMovie Theater is linked to your iCloud account. By default, iMovie applies a slow-motion setting to all imported clips so that you can slow down any movie clip in your movie project to create a special effect. If you link iMovie Theater to iCloud, you can set iMovie to automatically publish your finished movie projects to iMovie Theater so they can be viewed on other Apple devices like the iPad or iPod.

iMovie Theater and iCloud

iMovie Theater is a new feature of iMovie that stores your finished movies in one location and in a high-quality format. If you link Theater to iCloud, you can share your finished movies on other personal devices such as iPads or iPods as well as Apple TV.

1. Select iMovie, Preferences. The iMovie Preferences window displays.

2. Deselect the Apply Slow-Motion Automatically check box to turn off the default setting.

3. If you already have an iCloud account, select the Automatically Upload Content to iCloud check box to establish the connection between Theater and your iCloud account.

4. If you need to learn more about iCloud or would like to set up an iCloud account, click the Learn More link.

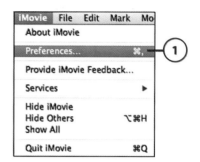

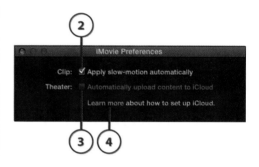

iCloud by Apple

Apple makes use of cloud technology through iCloud. When you create an iCloud account, you are setting up an online storage area that lets you connect multiple devices, like your iPhone, iPad, iPod, and desktop computer. You can easily share songs, movies, and photos from all your Apple devices without having to download files multiple times to each device. iCloud even keeps track of your devices so that if they are lost or stolen, iCloud lets you know where they are at. The initial 5GBs are free, and Apple offers other plans based on your storage needs. Learn more by visiting www.apple.com/icloud/.

Setting Movie Properties

Besides iMovie preferences, you also have default movie properties that are automatically applied to a movie project. These properties control how photos are placed in a movie, what theme is used, and the default duration time for clips and transitions. There are also properties for placement and control of automatic content, such as transitions and titles and automatically trimming your movie's background music to fit the movie's duration time.

1. Select the movie project that you want to edit by clicking All Projects from the Libraries list in the iMovie sidebar.

2. Select the movie project in the Event Browser. An overview of the movie properties is displayed above the Viewer as well as a Settings button.

Accessing Movie Properties for the Active Movie

You can quickly access the movie properties for the movie project you have active by choosing Window, Movie Properties. This displays the properties settings for the movie above the Viewer.

3. Click the Settings button to access the movie properties settings.

Overview of movie properties for selected movie project

My Movie Property Settings Disappeared!

If you move your mouse pointer down to the Project Browser while viewing movie properties settings, the settings disappear above the Viewer and are replaced with the clip image indicated by the playhead in the movie timeline. To display the movie properties again, repeat steps 1 and 2.

4. Select the placement setting for how photos are added to your movie project. Zoom applies the Ken Burns effect and creates a zoom into the photo. Crop automatically crops the photo to display in the movie frame dimensions. Fit automatically resizes the photo to display in the movie frame dimensions.

5. Select Automatic Content to set iMovie to automatically apply transitions and titles to the movie.

6. Click the Theme button to display the Themes window.

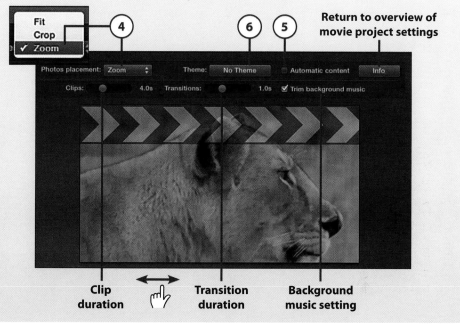

KEN BURNS EFFECT—WHAT'S THAT?

The Ken Burns Effect is a photography effect that slowly zooms in to a photo and pans left and right. This effect lets you focus on your subject in the photo as well as display individual elements of the photo in more detail. It's named after American director and producer of documentary films Ken Burns. He creates documentary films of historical events using archival footage and photographs to tell the story. He introduced a style for displaying photographs by slowly zooming in on the subject matter and panning from side to side within the photo. Ken Burns has been nominated for two Academy Awards, and he has won multiple Emmy Awards for his work. Apple incorporates the Ken Burns effect in iMovie, iPhoto, Aperture, and Final Cut Pro software.

>>>Go Further

7. Select a new theme. Click Change to apply a new theme to your movie project.

The Automatic Content Setting and Themes

If you just select a new theme and do not turn on Automatic Content, you will not see the new theme applied to your movie. You need to have the Automatic Content setting active to see your theme. To learn more about themes, see Chapter 8.

New theme applied   **Title indicators added to movie timeline**

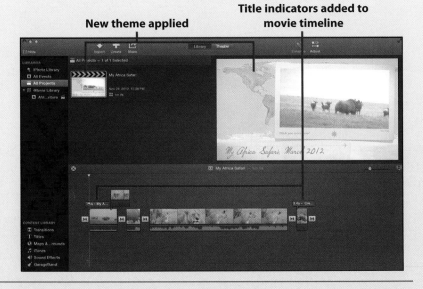

>>>Go Further

REMOVING A THEME FROM A MOVIE PROJECT

If you apply a theme to a movie project and later decide you want to remove it, you can. Access the movie properties settings so they display above the Viewer (refer to the "Accessing Movie Properties for the Active Movie" note earlier in this chapter) and then click the Theme button to display all movie themes. In the Themes window, select No Theme and click Change. Turn off the Automatic Content option in the movie properties settings by deselecting it. You also need to delete the theme titles created in the movie project above the movie timeline. Do this by selecting a title indicator from the timeline and then pressing Delete on your keyboard.

8. Click and drag the Clips slider left or right to adjust the default Clips duration time. The default setting is 4.0 seconds.

9. Click and drag the Transitions slider left or right to adjust the default Transitions duration time. The default setting is 1.0 seconds.

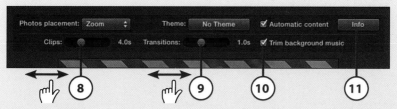

10. Select the Trim Background Music check box to automatically trim the background music to stop playing at the end of the movie. This stops the music wherever it is at when the movie video ends.

11. Click the Info button to return to the overview of the movie properties.

How iMovie Calculates Clip and Transition Duration

If you do not have a theme applied to your movie, iMovie automatically sets transitions to a default setting of .5 seconds for both the start of the clip and the end of the clip. If you have a theme applied, iMovie sets the transition to a default setting of 2 seconds for both the start and end of the clip. When you adjust either the Clips Zoom duration or the Transition duration setting, both settings are manipulated to accommodate for the shortest clip duration setting based on the movie project.

Playing the Entire Audio Track

If you want your movie music soundtrack to play all the way through even if the movie ends prior to the music ending, deselect the Trim Background Music check box in the movie properties settings. This allows you to display a photo image at the end of your movie for a visual display as the soundtrack finishes playing.

Default
iMovie
library with
many events

Clips
contained
in the Africa
2012 event

Additional
library
with
events

In this chapter, you find out about creating, organizing, and managing your iMovie libraries, events, and movie clips. You learn how to import movie clips as well as libraries and events created in older versions of iMovie. You also learn how to create new events and how to open other libraries from iPhoto or Aperture. Topics include the following:

2

→ Importing movie clips from your computer and from other devices

→ Updating libraries, events, and movie clips created in older versions of iMovie

→ Working with events and movie clips

→ Organizing libraries and events

→ Applying ratings to your movie clips

Importing and Organizing Video, Events, and Movie Clips

This chapter covers how to import your digital media into iMovie and how to organize your libraries, events, and movie clips. Your digital media can come from various devices, like a digital camera, iPhone or Android phone, iPad or other tablet device, iPod touch, or even FaceTime HD Camera. You also can import your existing media libraries and events that you created for use with older versions of iMovie. This chapter also explains how you can organize your libraries, events, and movie clips for easy browsing and finding of your media.

iMovie v10 Default Setup

When you first install iMovie v10, it automatically creates an empty event for the new iMovie workspace. An event is like a folder, and it can contain a single movie clip or multiple movie clips as well as iMovie movie projects, photos, and audio files. Because you have not created a new movie project yet, the iMovie workspace shows just the Library list, and the Event Browser displays in the lower half of the workspace. The Project Browser only displays when you have created your first movie project. iMovie v10 is ready for use, and the first step is to import video, audio, and photos into the iMovie Library.

**Default
iMovie library**

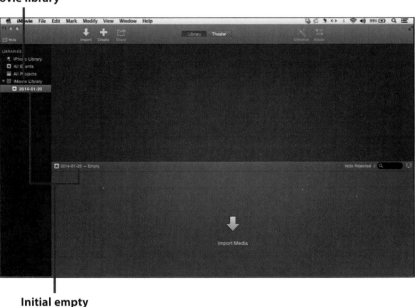

**Initial empty
event**

Update Events and Projects from Older Versions of iMovie

If you have used an older version of iMovie, when you open iMovie for the first time it automatically looks for existing iMovie events and movie projects on your computer. These would be any finalized iMovie events and movie projects created in an older version of iMovie so it can update them to work with iMovie v10. After being updated, they are automatically imported into the iMovie v10 Library.

1. When you first open iMovie v10, it automatically checks your computer for projects and events to update and then asks if you want to update now or later. Click Update.

Manually Updating Projects and Events from Older Versions

You can also select File, Update Projects and Events to initiate the update process for existing projects and events from older versions of iMovie.

2. After the updating process, you see your projects and events displayed in the Libraries list of the iMovie workspace.

3. Each event is marked with a star icon. Any movies that were finalized or shared are grouped in the Finalized Movies event, and the Updated Projects event holds all other previously created projects updated to the iMovie v10 format.

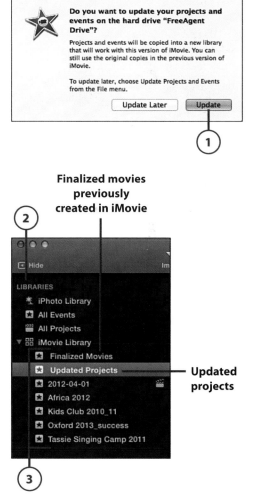

Do you want to update your projects and events on the hard drive "FreeAgent Drive"?

Projects and events will be copied into a new library that will work with this version of iMovie. You can still use the original copies in the previous version of iMovie.

To update later, choose Update Projects and Events from the File menu.

Update Later   Update

Finalized movies previously created in iMovie

LIBRARIES
- iPhoto Library
- All Events
- All Projects
- iMovie Library
  - Finalized Movies
  - Updated Projects — **Updated projects**
  - 2012-04-01
  - Africa 2012
  - Kids Club 2010_11
  - Oxford 2013_success
  - Tassie Singing Camp 2011

It's Not All Good

iMovie Quit During the Update Process!

Issues can occur during the update process. You might find that your iMovie suddenly quits or is interrupted during this process, or that it's taking a very long time. If this occurs, you don't have the most current version of iMovie v10. You need to update your iMovie v10 to v10.0.1 or later to solve this issue. To update iMovie to the latest version, open the App Store from System Preferences and click Check Now to update your Mac apps. You can then perform another iMovie update by selecting File, Upgrade Projects and Events.

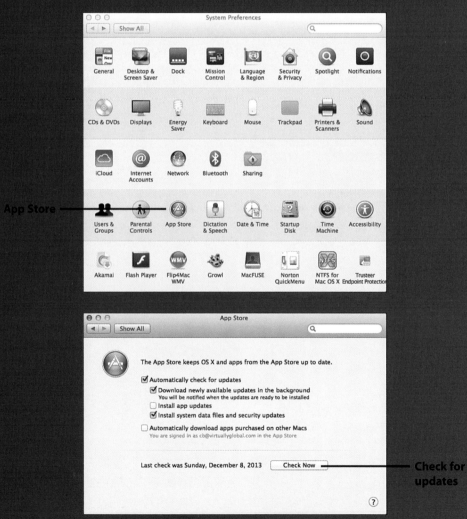

Update Events and Projects from an External Drive or Mobile Device

You can also update events and projects that are stored on an external drive or mobile device. The key to this is to make sure all the projects and events are located in the top level of the external drive or mobile device and then perform the update.

1. Attach the external drive to your computer.

2. Move all iMovie projects and events to the top-level of the external drive.

3. Open iMovie by double-clicking the iMovie icon on your desktop or by clicking it from the dock bar.

4. Choose File, Update Projects and Events.

Available devices

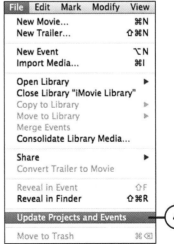

5. iMovie creates a new library file and updates and imports the existing projects and events into this new library.

iMovie Automatically Detects Events and Projects from Older Versions

When you attach another device and you already have iMovie open, it automatically searches the new device for existing projects and events. If it finds any that were created in an older version of iMovie, you see the Update Projects and Events message. Click Update and these projects and events are updated and imported into the iMovie Libraries list.

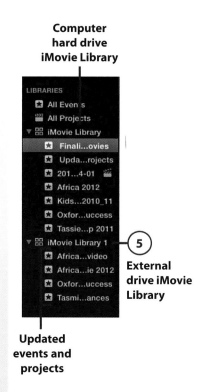

Computer hard drive iMovie Library

External drive iMovie Library

Updated events and projects

UNDERSTANDING THE UPDATE PROCESS

>>>Go Further

When you update your projects and events, iMovie looks for two folders—iMovie Events and iMovie Projects—to update their contents. To understand what is happening when you update events and projects, take a look at the new files and file structure that is created from the update process. Open your Finder and navigate to the drive that contains the iMovie Events folder and/or iMovie Projects folder that was updated. You see a couple of new files, an UpdateToiMovie10 and an iMovie Library file. The UpdateToiMovie10 file contains all the information for the iMovie Events or iMovie Projects folders to be used in iMovie v10, while keeping these two folders in their original format so they can still be used with older versions of iMovie. The iMovie Library file is the new library that works with iMovie v10. Any new or updated events and projects are now stored in the iMovie Library file. If you do not plan on using other versions of iMovie with your events and projects, you can delete the iMovie Events and Projects folders as the iMovie Library file now contains all the information you need for working with projects and events in iMovie v10.

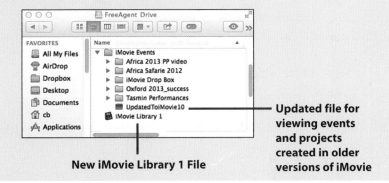

New iMovie Library 1 File

Updated file for viewing events and projects created in older versions of iMovie

It's Not All Good

Understanding the New iMovie Library File

After you update your projects and events, do not delete the new iMovie Library file as you are deleting all the projects and events for iMovie v10. You can delete the UpdateToiMovie10 file that contains the information for using projects and events from older versions of iMovie with iMovie v10. If you delete the UpdateToiMovie10 file and you decide you want to use the events and projects you created in older versions of iMovie in iMovie v10, you need to update these projects and events again to use with iMovie v10. If you don't plan on using older versions of iMovie, you can delete the UpdateToiMovie10 file as well as the actual iMovie Events or iMovie Projects folders as all files are now contained in the iMovie Library file.

Importing Movies from a Camera, Memory Card, and iMovie for iOS

iMovie can import movies from many different device types and file formats. You can use digital cameras, external drives, SAN disks, memory cards, flash drives, mobile phones, and tablets to import files to iMovie. You can even import movies, events, and projects from iMovie iOS. You can also record video directly into iMovie using your computer's built-in camera. Most Apple computers have preinstalled iSight for recording video through the computer's camera.

If you can make a wired or wireless connection between the device and your computer, and the movie is in an iMovie-supported format, you can import it to iMovie.

iMovie supports the following digital media file formats and codecs:

- QuickTime supported formats (MOV)
- Apple Encoded Video (M4V)
- Digital video (DV)
- DV Widescreen (AVCHD)
- High-definition recordings 1080i and 720p (either recorded at 25fps or 30fps) (HDV)
- Moving Picture Experts Group (MPEG-4 or simple profile MP4)
- 3G Mobile Phone Video (3GP)
- Advanced Audio Coding (AAC)
- Digital Audio Compression (AC3)
- Audio specific format by the Moving Picture Experts Group (MP3)
- Audio Interchange File Format (AIFF)

>>>Go Further

UNDERSTANDING DIGITAL VIDEO FILE FORMATS AND CODECS

There are two different technology concepts that make up digital video media formats: containers and codecs. At a basic understanding, digital video is made up of a combination of many pieces, such as video footage, audio, and metadata. A container is used to wrap all the pieces that make up the video and to communicate information about each piece of the file. Common containers are QuickTime (.mov), Flash (.flv), and MPEG-4 (MP4). The container also sets the codec. Codec is short for coder/decoder and establishes how to encode (or compress) and decode (or uncompress) the pieces. A container can hold many codecs. Different codecs work with different devices, so by having many codecs in the container, more devices can read the digital video. This topic is complex; to learn more about digital video file formats and codecs visit http://library.rice.edu/services/dmc/guides/video/VideoFormatsGuide.pdf.

iMovie and VOB File Format

iMovie cannot import video in the VOB (Video Object) file format. VOB is used for most DVD discs. There are third-party conversion applications that can convert the VOB file format to an iMovie-supported format. Search the Internet for more information about VOB and how to convert it to an iMovie-supported format.

Import New Media Files

After you have installed iMovie v10 and updated any events or projects from older versions of iMovie, you are ready to import new media into iMovie v10. You can import digital video, movies, audio files, and photos.

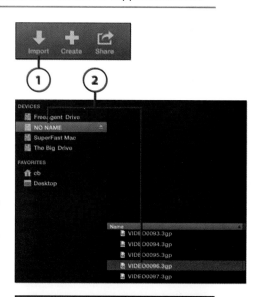

1. Click the Import button.

2. In the Import window, navigate to the device that has the movies, photo, audio, or video footage that you want to import. Click to select the movie or video.

3. Set where the video will be imported by clicking the Import To menu and selecting the appropriate menu choice from the menu. You can import to any iMovie Library, or directly into an existing event or you can create a new event.

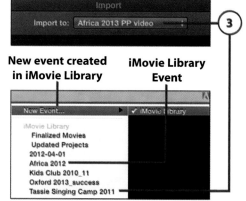

New event created in iMovie Library   **iMovie Library Event**

4. Select New Event if you want to import to a new event. When this is selected, the New Event window displays. Type a name and then click OK.

Using Click and Drag to Import Files

You can also click and drag a digital media file from the Finder into iMovie and drop it directly in a library or event in the Library list.

5. Click the Import Selected button to import movies and video into the iMovie Library.

6. The selected movies and video are now displayed as events in the Libraries list, and the movie clips that are in each event are displayed in the Event Browser.

>>>Go Further

SELECTING MULTIPLE FILES

You can select multiple files at one time by using the Shift or Command key. You can select adjacent files by clicking the first file in a list and then holding the Shift key while you click the last file in the list. All files between the first and last file are selected. You can also select nonadjacent files by clicking the first file and then holding the Command key from your keyboard as you click any other file you want. As long as the Command key is held, all files that you click are added to your selection.

Nonadjacent files

Adjacent files

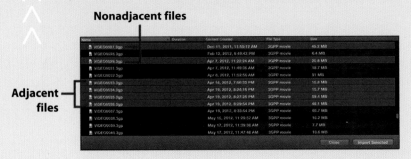

Importing New Media from an External Device

The process for importing video, audio, photos, or video footage from an external device is the same as importing files from your computer, you just need to navigate to the new media on the external device in step 2 of the "Import New Media Files" task.

What Is iMovie for iOS?

Apple also offers iMovie for iOS for use with iPad and iPod. This application is designed for mobile devices and enables you to quickly create movies and share them with others through iCloud and social media. Once shared, you can access them to download them to your computer and use them in your movie projects in iMovie. To learn more about iMovie for iOS, see Chapter 11, "Using iMovie On Your iPhone and iPad."

Importing from Other Libraries

iMovie can import entire events, photos, movies, and videos from other libraries. You can open a library created by an older version of iMovie or a library from iMovie v10. Then you can drag and drop entire events or movie clips into any other event or library listed in the iMovie Library list. iMovie even provides a direct link to the library used by iPhoto or Aperture in the Libraries list for quick access to media. Based on what you have installed on your computer, you see either iPhoto or Aperture in the Libraries list.

Import from iPhoto or Aperture

iMovie lets you easily import photos that you have in iPhoto or Aperture. iPhoto and Aperture are Apple's photo gallery products that enable you to store and edit your digital photos. If you use iPhoto or Aperture, you see a corresponding link in the Libraries list in iMovie.

Importing Audio Files from Other Libraries

You can also import audio files from other libraries used by GarageBand, Sound Effects, and the very popular iTunes.

Chapter 2

1. Click to select the iPhoto or Aperture Library in the Libraries list.

Overview of event media

2. Preview an iPhoto or Aperture Library event by hovering your mouse over it and moving the mouse to the left or right to skim the photos and movies in that event.

3. Double-click an event to display the photos and movies in the event.

4. If you chose the wrong event, click All Events from the drill-down path—all events of the iPhoto or Aperture Library display. Double-click the event you want.

Drill-down path   **Viewer displaying**
to event media   **selected clip**

File Structure of the Event Browser

You can return quickly to the event display in the Event Browser by clicking the All Events tab in the drill-down path at the top of the Event Browser.

---

5. Click and drag the photo or movie clip from the Event Browser to the destination event in the iMovie Library list.

Destination event   **Selected photo**

6. The photo or movie clip is imported into the destination event in the iMovie Library.

**Icon to visually identify
thumbnail as a photo**

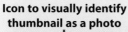

**Imported
photo**

Deleting Events, Movie Clips, and Photos

You can delete movie clips or photos from any event by right-clicking the movie clip or photo in the Event Browser and choosing Move to Trash from the context menu. You can delete entire events by selecting the event in the Libraries list, right-clicking and selecting Move to Trash.

Selected photo —

—— Move to Trash command

Import from Other Media Libraries

iMovie allows importing of events, audio files, and movie clips from other media libraries, like GarageBand, or from libraries created in older versions of iMovie. The key to this type of import is to be able to navigate to the library.

1. Connect the device that has the media library to your computer.

2. Choose File, Open Library, Other.

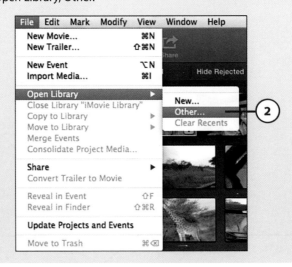

3. Click the Locate button in the Open Library window to open an existing library that you have not opened before.

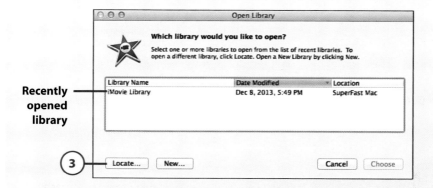

Recently opened library

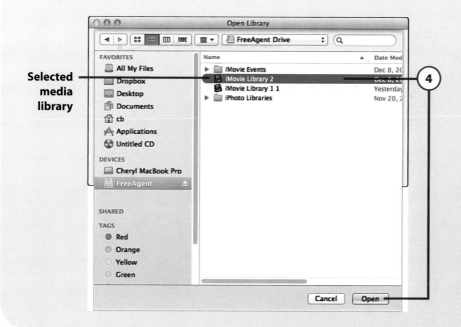

4. Navigate to the location of the media library and click it to select it. Then click Open. The library opens and displays in the Libraries list. The new media library events are listed, too.

Selected media library

5.   Click an event to select it.

New
library

⑤

6.   To import the entire event, click and drag the event to the Libraries list to import the entire event into the iMovie Library.

Destination
iMovie library

⑥

Selected event being
dragged to iMovie
library

Selected event

7. To import a movie clip, audio file, or photo from the event (not an entire event) to a library or an event, select the event in the new library by double-clicking it.

8. In the Event Browser, double-click to select the movie clip, audio file, or photo, and drag it to the event or library in the Libraries list. The movie clip, audio file, or photo is imported into the designated event or library.

Destination event

Image of movie clip being dragged to destination event

Selecting Multiple Movie Clips or Events

You can select more than one movie clip or event in the Event Browser by using the Command-click technique, or by clicking and dragging a selection rectangle through a group of movie clips and/or photos. As long as the rectangle touches any part of the movie clip/photo, it is included in the selection.

— **Selection rectangle**

— **Selected media**

Accessing Previously Opened Libraries

After you have opened a library, the next time you access the Open Library command—File, Open Library—any previously opened libraries are displayed in the Open Library window. To reopen a library that you have previously opened, click the library to select it and then click Choose.

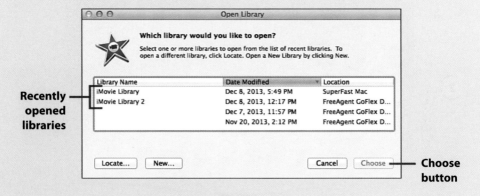

Recently opened libraries —

Choose button —

Where Is Imported Media from Another Library Stored?

If you use a movie clip or photo in your movie project, it is automatically added to the default iMovie Library. You do not need to import media from another library prior to using it in a movie project. You can access the media from the other library and place the media in your movie project.

Working with Events and Movie Clips

After you import your video and photos into iMovie, they are grouped and displayed as events in the Libraries list. An event is like a folder in which one or more clips, photos, or audio files are grouped based on recording date and time. The iMovie workspace provides a streamlined way to work with and organize events and movie clips. It allows for multiple ways to view, find, and select your media.

1. Click All Events in the Libraries list. The Event Browser displays all events in the libraries that you have opened in iMovie. Use the vertical scrollbar to scroll through all clips.

2. In the Event Browser, double-click an event to select it.

Vertical
scrollbar

3. The Event Browser displays all movie clips and photos for the selected event, and the Libraries list highlights the event.

All media in event

Viewing Library Event Media

You can select any opened library in the Libraries list, and the Event Browser displays all events contained in that library. You can also access all media in an event by selecting the event from the Libraries list, and the Event Browser displays all movie clips, photos, and audio files in the event.

4. Double-click a movie clip to select it; the Viewer displays the video.

**Viewer displays
movie**

Selecting a Movie Clip with a Shortcut
You can select an entire movie clip in the Event Browser by clicking the movie clip and then pressing X on your keyboard.

Previewing the Video of a Movie Clip
You can also position your mouse over any movie clip in the Event Browser, and the Viewer displays video footage of that movie clip. Move your mouse left or right (don't click), and you can skim through the clip.

Play a Movie Clip

iMovie makes it easy to preview the video of a movie clip. You have different techniques available for what video to play back in a movie clip. You can play the clip from the beginning or you can play just a selection of the clip. This enables you to quickly preview any video in your clips.

1. Select an event from the Libraries list by clicking it.

2. To preview your movie clip from the beginning, select a movie clip in the Event Browser by double-clicking it to select the entire clip.

3. The Viewer displays the movie clip video. Move your mouse into the Viewer and the playback options display.

4. Click the Play button to play the movie clip from the beginning.

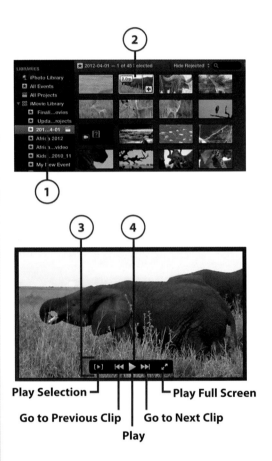

Play Selection

Play Full Screen

Go to Previous Clip

Go to Next Clip

Play

Manually Initiating Playback Options

You can also manually initiate playback options through menu bar commands or through keystrokes from your keyboard. To use a command, choose View and then select one of the playback menu commands. Notice that the keystroke for the command is listed to the right of the menu command. If you press any of these associated keystrokes, you initiate that playback command.

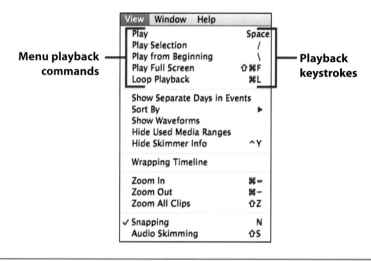

Menu playback commands

Playback keystrokes

CONTROLLING PLAYBACK

To advance through your movie clips by previewing them, you can use the Go to Previous Clip or Go to Next Clip buttons. When clicked, these options either select the previous or the next clip in the Event Browser based on the clip that you have selected.

To stop playback, simply press the spacebar on your keyboard. Press the spacebar again to continue playing the clip.

If you click Play Full Screen, the Viewer expands to fill your monitor screen. To exit Full-Screen mode, press the Esc key on your keyboard.

Select Part of a Movie Clip

Another playback option that is very useful is to play just part of a clip.

1. Select an event from the Libraries list by clicking it.

2. Position your mouse inside the movie clip and then click and drag to select a portion of the clip.

3. Move your mouse into the Viewer and click the Play Selection button in the playback options. The Viewer plays only the selected portion of the movie clip based on the starting frame and the ending frame of the selection.

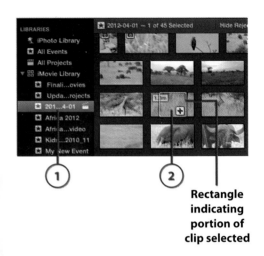

Rectangle indicating portion of clip selected

Use the Skimmer and Playhead

Another technique for previewing your movie clips is to use the skimmer and playhead for quick review of the video. The playhead is used to set where the movie begins playing. The skimmer lets you quickly skim through the clip content by just moving your mouse.

1. Select an event from the Libraries list by clicking it.

2. In the Event Browser, hover your mouse over a clip. You will see an orange vertical line in the clip based on the location of your mouse. This is the skimmer.

Time indicator   **Skimmer**

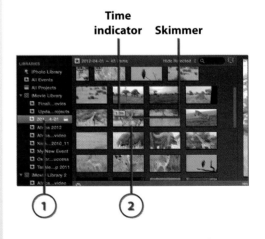

Manually Playing a Movie Clip

To play a movie clip from the position of the playhead, press the spacebar on your keyboard. The Viewer displays the video of the movie clip.

3. Move your mouse left or right in the parameter of the clip and the Viewer displays a quick preview of the video footage by skimming through the frames. This is called skimming.

4. Click to set the playhead at a specific frame in the video of the clip.

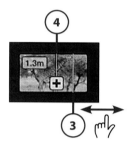

5. The Viewer displays the movie based on where the playhead is positioned in the movie. Click Play to begin playing the clip based on the position of the playhead in the movie.

Stepping Through a Movie Clip Frame by Frame

You might find that skimming is great, but not quite precise enough to select the exact starting frame of a clip you want. You can step through a video frame-by-frame using the left-arrow and right-arrow keys on your keyboard. First click to set the playhead in a movie clip, and then press the left- or right-arrow key to move the playhead one frame at a time to the exact location you want in the video. The Viewer displays this frame-by-frame progression through the video.

Locate a Movie File

There might be times when you need to find where a movie clip is located on your computer or on an attached device. You can do this through a menu command.

1. Select an event in the Libraries list.

2. In the Event Browser, select a movie clip by double-clicking it.

3. Select File, Reveal in Finder.

4. A Finder window is displayed with the movie clip file highlighted.

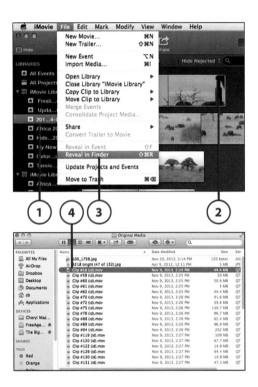

Getting Organized

As you might guess, when you start working with iMovie, things can get pretty cluttered because of multiple libraries opened and many events, movie clips, photos, and audio files available. You would quickly get confused and frustrated without some organization techniques that are included with iMovie. You can quickly find any movie clip through a search feature, and you can rename any event or library. You can create events for grouping similar clips together as well as combining and arranging clips and projects by copying, moving, or deleting them. You can also merge events so that all movie clips in the events are combined into one event.

Rename a Library or Event

Sometimes it is helpful to rename a library or event so that it visually provides more information about the media contents.

1. Click the library or event to select it from the Libraries list.

2. Click again on the name of the library or event to access the rename text box. Type a new name for the library or event.

Create a New Event

There are other times when you will want to create a new event and organize your movie clips that have a similar theme into this new event.

1. Select the library you want the event to be associated with from the Libraries list.

2. Right-click the library and choose New Event from the context menu. You can also select File, New Event.

3. A new event is displayed under the selected library. Type a new name for the event in the rename text box.

4. Click the Import Media button in the Event Browser to import new movies and video. Alternatively, you can click and drag movie clips from other events into your new event.

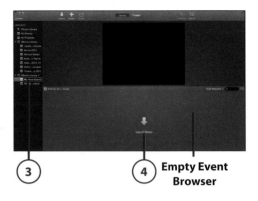

③   ④ **Empty Event Browser**

Deleting an Event or Movie Clip

You can delete an event or movie clip by right-clicking it and choosing Move Event to Trash (if you are deleting an event) or Move Clip to Trash (if you are deleting a movie clip). The event or movie clip is deleted from the iMovie Library but still resides on your hard drive in the iMovie Events folder.

Rearrange Events Between Libraries

iMovie is a great video library platform, meaning if you want you can use it to organize your video and movies as a video library. Events can be rearranged between libraries.

1. Select the event or events to rearrange and drag them on top of a library. The event or events are moved to the destination library.

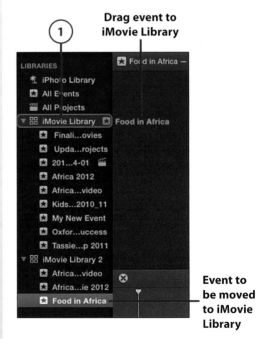

① **Drag event to iMovie Library**

Event to be moved to iMovie Library

Copying an Event or Movie Clip

You can copy events and movie clips to other libraries or events by holding down the Option key while you drag the event or movie clips to the destination library or event. This creates a copy of the event or movie clip in the destination library or event rather than moving it.

2. You can also rearrange movie clips between events by clicking and dragging a movie clip from the Event Browser to a new event in the Libraries list.

Merge Events

You can merge two or more events to combine the contained media files into one event.

1. In the Libraries list, select the events to be merged by using the Shift-click technique to select adjacent events, or by using the Command-click technique to select nonadjacent events.

2. Select File, Merge Events.

Using the Context Menu to Merge Events

You can also find the Merge Events command by right-clicking one of the selected events in the Libraries list and choosing Consolidate Event Media.

Consolidate Event Media command

Rating Movie Clips

Another way you can organize your movie clips is to apply a rating to them. You have a choice of rating your movie clips either as a favorite or as rejected. After you have rated your clips, you can then search for your favorite clips or you can hide all rejected movie clips.

1. Select an event from the Libraries list.

2. In the Event Browser, select a movie clip by double-clicking it.

3. Right-click the clip and choose one of the two ratings from the menu, Favorite or Reject.

   • Choose Favorite and the thumbnail of the movie clip displays a horizontal green line indicating that the Favorite rating has been applied.

   • Choose Reject and the thumbnail of the movie clip displays a horizontal red line indicating that the Reject rating has been applied.

Using Menubar Commands to Rate Events or Movie Clips

You can also use the Favorite or Reject commands from the Mark menu to rate events and movie clips.

Rating Multiple Events

You can apply a rating to multiple events by using the Command-click technique to select multiple movie clips in the Event Browser and then select Mark, Favorite or Mark, Reject.

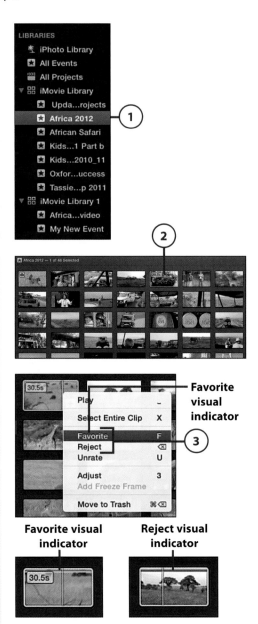

Favorite visual indicator

Favorite visual indicator

Reject visual indicator

4. Use the filter feature of iMovie to filter your movie clips by rating. Select a library or event to search from the Library list.

The Filter by Rating Menu Default Setting

The default setting for the Filter By Rating menu is All Clips. This setting displays all events in a library or all movie clips and media contained in an event.

5. Click the Filter By Rating menu to display the four filter options.

- Choose Favorites and the Event Browser displays only the clips rated Favorite for the selected library or event.

- Choose Rejected and the Event Browser displays only the clips rated Reject for the selected library or event.

- Choose Hide Rejected to hide all rejected clips for the selected library or event.

- Choose All Clips to remove the filter and display all movie clips in the Event Browser.

Filter by rating

Filter of Favorites applied

Favorite rated clips

Filter of Rejected applied

Reject rated clips

6. To remove a rating applied to a clip, select the clip in the Event Browser, right-click the clip, and select Unrate or choose Mark, Unrate from the menu bar.

Search for Tags Applied in Previous Versions of iMovie

In previous versions of iMovie, you could apply a custom tag to a movie clip. The tag let you label your clips with anything you wanted. In iMovie v10, movie clips can't be tagged, but you can still search your updated movie clips from previous versions of iMovie based on keywords that you have applied in that older version of iMovie.

1. Select a library or event from the Libraries list.

2. Make sure that no ratings filters have been applied by choosing All Clips from the Search By Rating menu.

3. The Event Browser displays all clips for the selected library or event. Type a keyword into the Search text box and the Event Browser displays all clips tagged with this keyword.

Movie tagged with keyword

Event with linked project   Movie clips   Project Browser
                                    in event   with movie
                                                         timeline

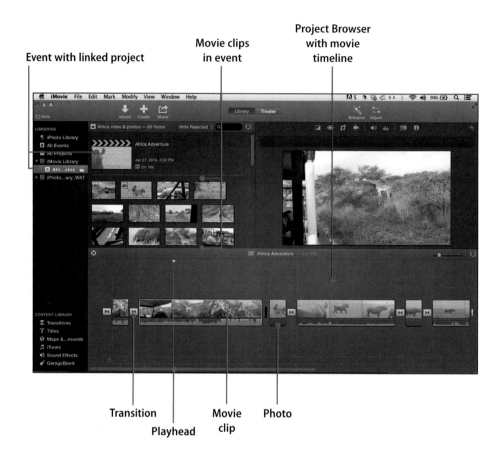

Transition   Movie   Photo
          Playhead clip

In this chapter, you find out how to create a new movie project and add clips and photos to the movie. You also apply transitions and special effects for a more polished presentation of your movie. Topics include the following:

→ Creating a new movie project
→ Adding clips to your movie
→ Adding transitions between clips in your movie
→ Adding special effects to a photo or clip
→ Adding photos to your movie

Creating a New Movie Project

A movie in iMovie can be made up of lots of elements: movie clips, photos, audio, sound effects, titles, and transitions. iMovie represents a movie as a project. The project contains all your movie elements for the new movie, and automatically keeps track of all these elements. You can have multiple projects in iMovie.

Creating a New Movie Project

To create a new iMovie project, you first create a new movie.

1. Choose File, New Movie or click the Create button in the toolbar and choose Movie. The Themes window displays.

2. Select the theme you want to use. If you don't want to use a preexisting theme, select the No Theme option and then click Create.

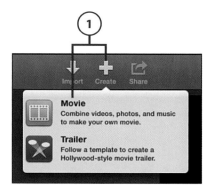

New Themes

Themes have been available in all versions of iMovie. Themes help you quickly create a stylish movie—the theme has the design layout and design elements created for the movie. You can add your own movie clips, transitions, photos, audio, movie titles, and subtitles. iMovie v10 has 16 movie themes to choose, and Apple added 8 new themes in the iMovie for iOS product, which is part of iMovie v10 download. See Chapter 11, "Using iMovie on Your iPhone and iPad," to learn how to use iMovie for iOS.

No Theme

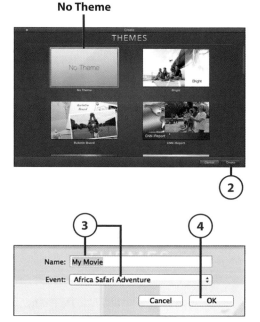

3. Name your new movie project and select the event you want to use for the movie.

iMovie and Events

Don't worry if you don't have all your clips or events available when you create a new movie. You can import media files, video footage, and audio files anytime by choosing File, Import Media, or by clicking the Import button from the toolbar.

4. Click OK to create your new movie project.

5. Your new movie is created and the iMovie Library displays the event with a new movie icon to the right indicating that a project is attached to that event.

6. To see your project, click All Projects in the Libraries list.

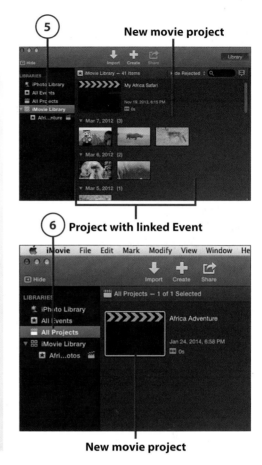

New movie project

Project with linked Event

New movie project

Adding Clips to Your Movie Project

After you have a new movie project created and events imported into the iMovie Library, you can add clips and other media to your movie. You place them in the order that you want for your movie, and then edit them to create the sequence and flow of your movie. You can also add photos and audio files that display as audio waveforms in the timeline.

Aspect Ratios and iMovie

Aspect ratio is the size of the screen for the digital video—its width and height. The default aspect ratio for a movie project in iMovie is 16:9, and you cannot change it. If you add a clip to the timeline with a different aspect ratio, like 4:3, iMovie automatically adjusts the ratio to 16:9 by cropping the clip. You can adjust the cropping to change what is shown in the clip. To learn more about cropping, see Chapter 4, "Editing and Correcting Movie Clips."

1. If you do not have a project open, click All Projects in the Library list.

2. Double-click the Movie Project in the Event Browser to open the movie timeline. The Event Browser displays the clips tied to the event used when you created your movie project.

3. Click the Adjust Thumbnail Appearance button to adjust the thumbnail of the clips.

4. Click the Clip Size slider and drag it to the left to decrease the thumbnail image size. Drag to the right to increase the clip thumbnail image size.

5. Click and drag the Zoom duration slider to the left and set it to All. Dragging the Zoom slider to the left decreases the amount of footage seen in a clip thumbnail; dragging to the right increases the amount of footage. Set the Zoom slider to All to see small thumbnail images of all clips in an event.

Scrolling Through Clips in an Event

You can scroll through all the clips in an event by dragging the vertical scrollbar up and down in the Event Browser.

6. Select the entire clip in the Event Browser either by double-clicking the clip or by clicking a clip and then pressing X on your keyboard.

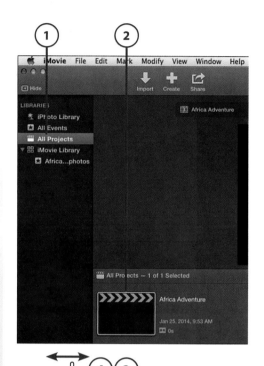

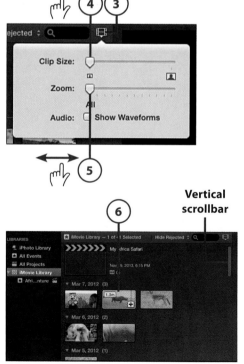

Selecting a Portion of a Clip

You can choose just part of the clip in the Event Browser by clicking and dragging a portion of the clip to select it. To increase the size of the thumbnail image as well as the amount of video displayed in the thumbnail, click the Adjust Thumbnail Appearance button and set the Clip Size and Zoom duration settings.

Selected 13.5 seconds of footage from active clip

7. Drag the clip to a location in the movie timeline. When you see the green plus sign icon display, release the mouse button and the clip is added to the movie timeline. Alternatively, you can add the movie to the last frame in the timeline by clicking the Add the Selection to Movie button in the active clip.

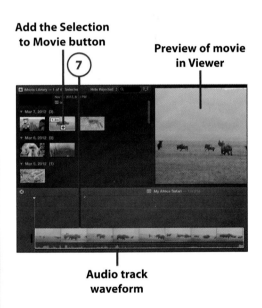

Add the Selection to Movie button

Preview of movie in Viewer

Audio track waveform

Adding a Clip to the Timeline

When you drag a movie clip to the timeline, it takes iMovie a few seconds to process the video of the clip into the timeline. When it is processed, you see a green plus sign icon in the clip. Now let go of the drag by releasing your mouse button. If you release the button before you see the green plus sign, the clip is not inserted into the timeline.

Identifying the Movie Clips in Your Movie Project

After you add a clip to a movie project, the Event Browser displays the thumbnail of the clip with an orange line at the bottom of the clip. This lets you easily distinguish clips that are used in the project with those that have not been used.

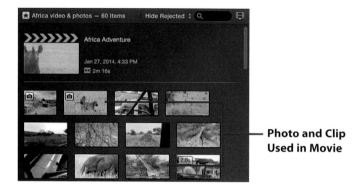

— **Photo and Clip Used in Movie**

Often you will have many clips and photos in the movie timeline. Finding the clip used for the project in the Event Browser could be a tough process, especially if you have a lot of libraries, events, and clips. iMovie makes this easy. To reveal a clip in the Browser from a clip in the movie timeline, right-click the timeline clip and choose Reveal in Event from the context menu.

Selected clip —

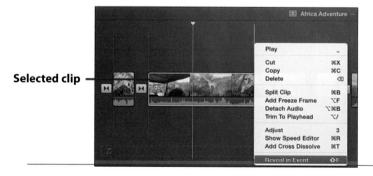

>>>Go Further

SELECTING MULTIPLE CLIPS IN THE BROWSER

You can select a group of adjacent clips by double-clicking the first clip in the group and then holding the Shift key as you single-click the last clip in the group. All clips between the first and last are selected.

You can add multiple nonadjacent clips by using the Command-click technique: Double-click the first clip in the Browser to select it and then hold the Command key on your keyboard and single-click other clips to add to your selection.

— Selection of four adjacent clips

— Selection of four nonadjacent clips

Rearrange Clips in the Movie Timeline

As you develop your movie timeline with clips and photos, you might need to rearrange the order in which the clips are placed.

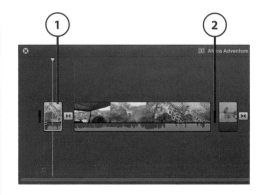

1. Select a clip in the movie timeline by clicking it.

2. Click and drag the selected clip before or after another clip in the movie timeline. Place it on the vertical placement bar that is between each clip.

3. iMovie adjusts the movie timeline so you can drop the clip in place.

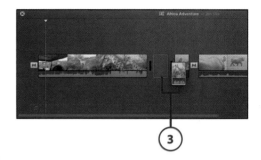

3

Replace a Clip in the Movie Timeline

You can also replace a clip in the movie timeline with another clip from the Event Browser.

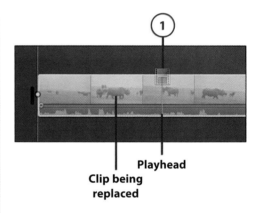

1

1. Click and drag a new clip from the Event Browser and place it on top of a clip in the movie timeline.

2. The context menu displays—choose one of the following options.

   - Choose Replace to replace the entire clip.

   - Choose Replace from Start to replace the selected clip video from the start of the clip to the location of the playhead.

   - Choose Replace from End to replace the clip video from the playhead to the end of the clip.

   - Choose Insert to insert the clip into the clip at the location of the playhead.

Playhead

Clip being replaced

2

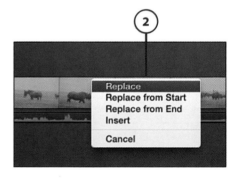

Delete Clips in the Movie Timeline

To delete a clip that you have added to your movie timeline, just click to select the clip in the timeline and press the Delete key on your keyboard.

>>>Go Further

CREATING A CUTAWAY CLIP

You can also position clips so that one is above the other and they overlap each other in the movie timeline; this is called a *cutaway clip*. This creates a way to show additional information about a clip. For instance, if the main clip is about your child's orchestra performance, you can show your child playing and then cut away to a view of the entire orchestra. See Chapter 5, "Adding Special Effects, Maps, Backgrounds, and Titles," for more information about cutaway clips.

Cutaway clip ———

Adding Clip Transitions

As you gain skill developing your movies, you will use multiple clips and photos for your movies. Each clip is positioned in the movie timeline and they play sequentially, with an abrupt change between each clip. Transitions are used to create smooth transitions between your clips. iMovie has 24 preset transitions that you can use in your movie. You can add transitions manually to your clips or you can have iMovie automatically add one transition between all clips in your movie.

If you are using a theme for your movie, the theme style transitions are displayed above the standard iMovie transitions displayed in the Event Browser.

1. Click Transitions in the Content Library in the iMovie sidebar.

2. The Browser displays all transitions. Click a transition to select it.

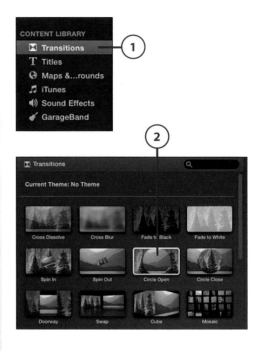

Clip Transitions

You can view the clip transition prior to placing it in your movie. To preview a clip transition, select the clip transition in the Browser, and then move your mouse pointer from the left edge of the selected transition to the right. The Skimmer displays as you move your mouse pointer, and the Viewer displays the video as you skim through the video in the transition.

3. Drag the transition from the Browser and place it between two sequential clips in your movie's timeline. When you see the green plus sign indicating that iMovie has processed the transition, release your mouse button to insert the transition between the clips.

Skimmer

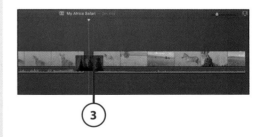

4. The Transition icon displays between your clips to indicate that a transition has been applied.

5. Click the Transition icon in the movie timeline to display the transition in the Viewer.

6. To use this transition for all other transitions set in your movie, double-click the Transition icon to access the Settings toolbar above the Viewer.

7. Click Apply to All Transitions if you want to apply the transition to any other transition you have set for your clips in your movie.

Deleting Transitions

To delete an applied transition, select it in the timeline and press the Delete key on your keyboard.

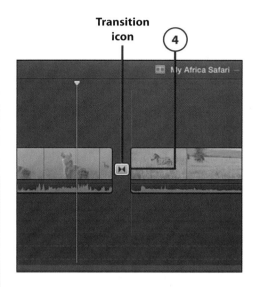

Transition icon (4)

(5)

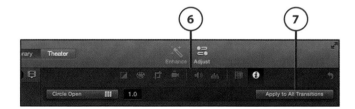
(6) (7)

Switch Transitions

You can switch or replace a transition that you've set in your movie's timeline to a different transition.

1. Click Transitions in the Content Library of the iMovie sidebar.

2. Click and drag a new transition from the Browser to the Transition icon in the movie timeline. The new transition replaces the applied transition.

3. The Viewer window displays the new transition effect in the Clip.

Edit Transition Duration Time

You can increase or decrease the duration of the transition. iMovie automatically applies one-half of the transition time to both adjacent clips. If either clip is too short to accommodate this new duration time, iMovie automatically adjusts the duration to the maximum amount possible based on the adjacent clips. The default transition is set to 2 seconds, so the transition for the beginning of the clip is set to 1 second, and the remaining 1 second is applied to the transition at the end of the clip.

1. Double-click the Transition icon in the movie's timeline to display the transition settings above the Viewer.

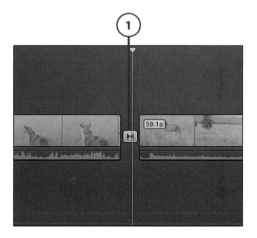

2. Double-click the Duration Setting field and enter the time duration you want for the transition. Press Return to apply this new duration setting.

Don't Forget to Return

You must press Return after typing in the new duration setting. If you do not press Return, the new duration is not applied and the old duration is used.

Fade to Transitions

You can also cause a movie or a photo to fade to different renditions of a clip. You have a choice of Black and White, Sepia, or Dream. A fade to Black and White causes the clip to transition from full color to black and white. A fade to Sepia causes the clip to transition from full color to sepia color, and the Dream setting creates a transition to a sepia version of the clip with a halo effect, which gives it a dreamlike quality.

1. Select the clip to which you want to apply a fade to transition.

2. Choose Modify, Fade To and then select one of the three transition effects.

Adding Photos to Your Movie

You can add still photos to your movie. You can add a photo from iPhoto or Aperture because they now share a common library. You can also create a freeze frame in a clip by freezing a frame and then inserting that frame into your movie. If you do not have iPhoto or Aperture, you can add photos from any location or device that can connect to your computer.

Default iPhoto
Library

Viewer image of
selected photo

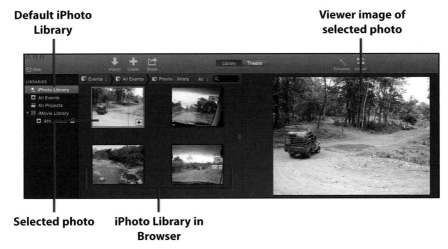

Selected photo

iPhoto Library in
Browser

Add a Photo from iPhoto/Aperture

iMovie and iPhoto/Aperture work hand in hand when it comes to adding photos to your movie. Built in to the iMovie sidebar is a link to your iPhoto/Aperture Library, which displays your photo library by events. You can view Events and apply filters through the Events menu. Based on how you have iPhoto/Aperture set up, the search menu displays any of these available options: Faces, Places, Albums, Facebook, Flickr, or iCloud.

1. Click iPhoto/Aperture Library.

2. Double-click the event that contains the photo you want to add to the movie. You can view by Events, Faces, Places, Albums, Facebook, Flickr, or iCloud.

Skimming Through an iPhoto Event

You can skim through photos. Select the event in the Browser and then move the mouse left or right. The photos contained in the event display from the first to the last.

3. Click the photo you want to use.

4. Click the Add to Movie button or choose Edit, Add to Movie. The photo is inserted at the end of your movie.

5. Alternatively, click and drag the photo to any location in the movie timeline. Do not release your mouse button until you see the green plus sign icon that indicates that iMovie has processed the photo insert and it can be dropped into the movie timeline.

Access photo by Events, Faces, and Albums

(2)

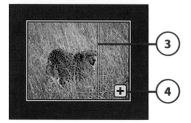

(3)
(4)

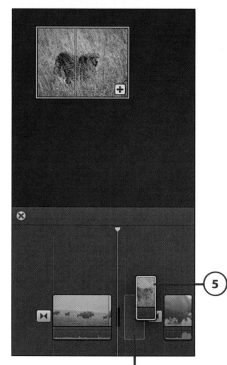

(5)

Placement of clip indicator

Using a Photo as a Cutaway Image

You can use a photo as a cutaway image. Drag the photo from the Event Browser above a clip in the movie timeline. You can also drag an already placed photo from the movie timeline above another clip in the timeline.

First frame indicator

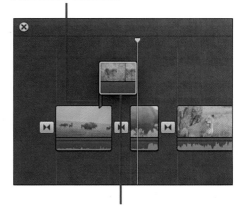

Selected photo placed as cutaway image

Add a Freeze-Frame Image

iMovie can also capture a still image from a clip. This is called freezing a frame. You can then use the freeze frame in your movie.

1. Click to position the playhead in your movie timeline on the frame of the image you want to capture.

2. Choose Modify, Add Freeze Frame or right-click the clip and choose Add Freeze Frame from the context menu.

Preview of frame

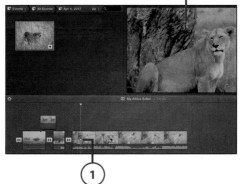

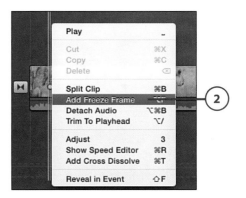

3. iMovie creates a photo of the freeze frame at the location of the playhead, splitting the movie clip into two pieces. You can now add transitions or relocate the photo by dragging it to a new location in the timeline.

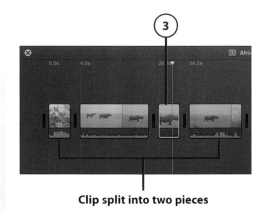

Clip split into two pieces

Using the Flash and Hold Effect

Another effect that is similar to a Freeze Frame is the Flash and Hold effect. This effect applies a fade-to-white effect to the selected clip. The last frame of the clip is then converted to a freeze frame with the Ken Burns effect automatically applied to the freeze-frame image. (Read more about the Ken Burns effect later in this chapter.) To apply the Flash and Hold effect, select a clip and choose Modify, Flash and Hold Last Frame.

Use Multiple iPhoto Libraries

You can have multiple iPhoto Libraries opened and accessible in iMovie.

1. Choose File, Open Library, Other. This displays a window with options for opening a library in iMovie. Click Locate.

2. Navigate to an existing iPhoto Library and then click Open.

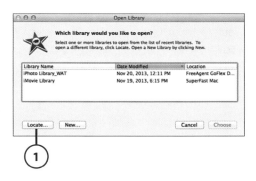

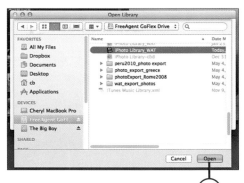

3. The new iPhoto Library displays in the iMovie Library list.

4. Click the new iPhoto Library to display the events and clips it contains.

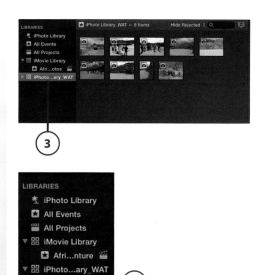

Add Photos from Anywhere

You can import a photo from any connection on your computer. This could be your local hard drive, an external drive, or iCloud. If your computer can connect to it, you can import from it.

1. Click File, Import Media.

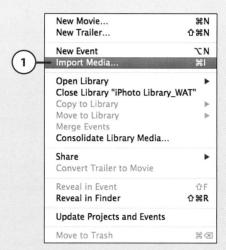

2. Navigate to the device or location of the new photo. Select the photo.

**Location of
photo to import**

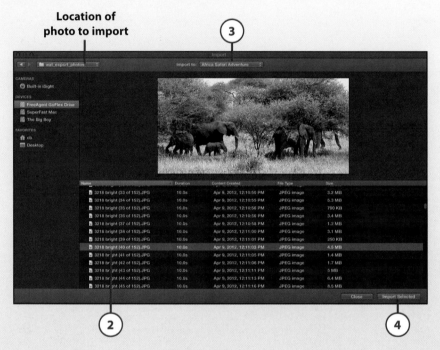

3. Click the Import To menu and select the event you want to import the photo to.

4. Click Import Selected.

Customize the Ken Burns Effect

When you add a photo to your movie, the Ken Burns effect is automatically applied. The Ken Burns effect is an animated zoom of the photo, and it is a very popular way to show-case an image. iMovie lets you customize this effect.

1. Click to select a photo in the timeline and then click the Adjust button above the Viewer.

Initiating the Adjust Toolbar with a Right-Click
You can also access the Adjust Toolbar by right-clicking a clip in the timeline and choosing Adjust from the context menu.

2. Click the Crop button.

3. Click the Ken Burns button.

Start frame

End frame

4. Adjust the Start frame and/or End frame size by clicking inside either the Start or End frame to make that frame active. Then resize the active frame by dragging any of the corners of the frame to make it larger or smaller.

5. Adjust the Start and/or End frame position in the photo by clicking in the middle of the frame and dragging left, right, up, or down. iMovie adds an arrow indicator to show the new position of the frame in relation to the other frame.

Click and drag frame to new location

6. Click the Apply Crop Adjustment button to apply the revised Ken Burns effect.

7. Click the Remove Crop Adjustment button to revert the clip to its original format.

Applying the Ken Burns Effect to Clips

You can also apply the Ken Burns effect to a clip. Instead of first selecting a photo, select a clip in the movie timeline and then follow the steps for "Customize the Ken Burns Effect."

Turn Off Automatic Effects

By default, iMovie automatically applies the Ken Burns effect to any inserted photos. You can turn this off so that photos are inserted in their normal static state.

1. Choose Window, Movie Properties to display movie properties above the Viewer.

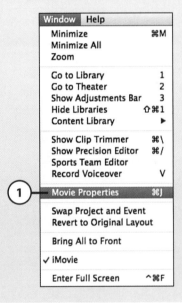

2. Click the Settings button.

3. Deselect the Automatic Content button in the Movie Settings view.

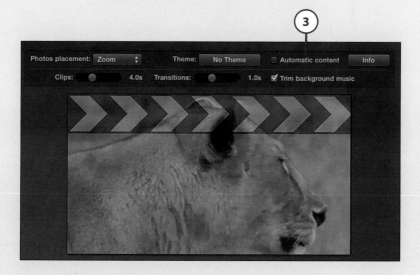

Starting
frame   Playhead

Ending
frame

Image of video
based on location
of playhead or
skimmer

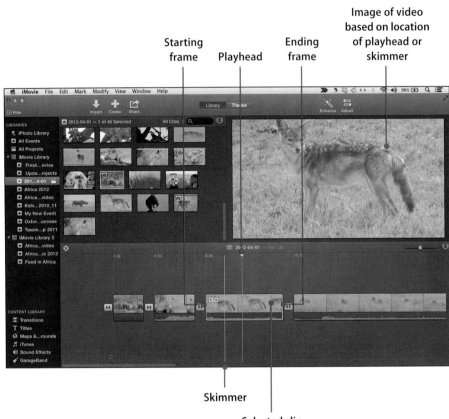

Skimmer

Selected clip
in timeline

In this chapter, you find out how to modify your clips in a movie project by editing and correcting the clips in their duration or orientation as well as correcting video that is shaky or blurry. Topics include the following:

→ Trimming clips

→ Adjusting starting and ending frames with the Clip Trimmer

→ Using the Precision Editor

→ Correcting video that is shaky or blurry

→ Splitting a movie clip into two clips

→ Deleting clips

→ Rotating clips

Editing and Correcting Movie Clips

As you develop your movie project in iMovie, you'll find that you need more control over the clips in the movie timeline. iMovie has advanced editing tools that enable you to precisely control the duration and orientation of the clip and to correct problems with the recorded video. You can quickly delete or rotate clips in the timeline and split a movie clip into two clips. iMovie can also correct shaky or blurry video caused by the camera being moved too quickly when recording the video.

Trimming Movie Clips

When you adjust the starting and ending frames of the movie clips in the timeline, you are trimming a clip. iMovie lets you zero in on a frame-by-frame view of your video so that you can precisely set your starting and ending frames for each clip in the movie timeline.

When you select a clip in the timeline, iMovie displays a skimmer and a play-head for previewing and playing the video. Use the skimmer to preview your clips frame-by-frame, and then set the exact starting and ending frames for your clip and trim the clip. iMovie has a few different ways to trim a clip. One way is to trim the clip directly in the movie timeline.

Trimming a Clip in the Timeline Doesn't Affect Linked Clip in Event

When you add a clip to the timeline, it maintains a link to the original clip that is grouped in an event in the Library list. Any trimming of the video is only to the clip in the movie timeline; the original video is still intact where it is stored on your computer. If you want to trim the original video, you need to do this on the recording device where the video was first recorded.

---

1. Add a clip from the Event Browser to the movie timeline by double-clicking a clip to select it in the Event Browser, and then dragging it into the movie timeline.

2. In the movie timeline, select the clip to trim by clicking it.

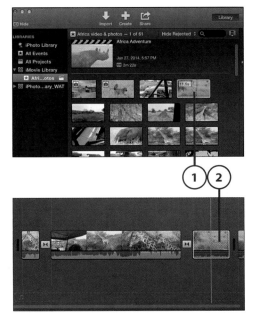

3. Move your mouse pointer anywhere in the selected clip and
the skimmer displays. Move your
mouse pointer left or right (don't
click and drag) to skim through
the video. The Viewer displays the
video as you skim through the
video of the clip.

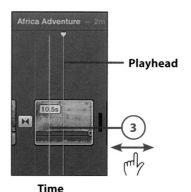

Playhead

Time adjustment

Using the Arrow Keys to Skim Through a Clip

Click to set the playhead at a specific location in the selected clip.
Then press the left- or right-arrow
keys on your keyboard to advance
one frame at a time through the
video.

4. To adjust the starting or ending frame of the movie, position
the mouse pointer on the left
or right border of the clip. The
pointer becomes the Trim tool, as
indicated by the double-headed
arrow. Click and drag to the left
or right to adjust the starting or
ending frame of the clip. A time
adjustment displays indicating
the amount of time you are deleting or adding.

Adjusting the Clip Display Size for More Precise Trimming

Use the Zoom In or Out on Clips
slider in the Project Browser to
increase the view of the clip you
are trimming for more precise
edits to the video in a clip.

Zoom In or Out on Clips slider

Use the Clip Trimmer

To precisely edit a clip in the movie timeline, iMovie has the Clip Trimmer tool. The Clip Trimmer edits clips frame-by-frame so you can set exact starting and ending frames for your video.

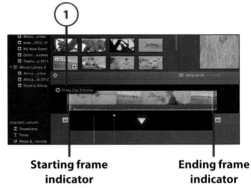

1. Double-click a clip in the Project Browser to display the Clip Trimmer.

Starting frame indicator   **Ending frame indicator**

2. Skim the video of the clip by moving the mouse pointer into the Clip Trimmer so the skimmer displays. Move the pointer left or right to skim the video of the clip. The Viewer displays the video.

3. Position the mouse pointer on either the left or right border of the clip. This displays the Trim tool. Click and drag left or right to adjust the starting or ending frame of the clip.

4. To adjust what video is shown in the trimmed clip, move your mouse to the center of the trimmed clip, then click and drag left or right to reposition the clip's video to the new duration created by the starting and ending frames. Your pointer turns to a double-arrow filmstrip tool.

5. When you have the clip trimmed as you want, close the Clip Trimmer by clicking the Close Clip Trimmer button.

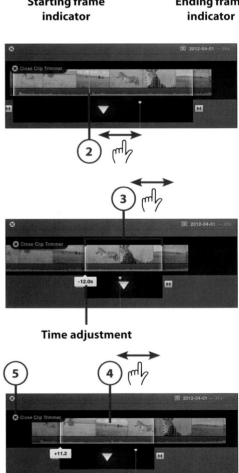

Time adjustment

6. The movie timeline displays the trimmed clip.

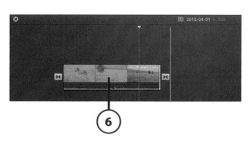

Trimming a Clip to the Playhead

You can trim a clip in the timeline based on the location of the playhead. Position the playhead where you want the movie to start and then choose Modify, Trim to Playhead.

Trim to Playhead command

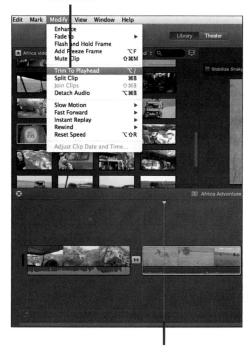

Playhead

Use the Precision Editor

iMovie also has the Precision Editor for making frame-by-frame edits to a clip to set a precise duration of the video for the clip. It is similar to the Clip Trimmer as it lets you fine-tune the starting and ending frames of your movie but with even more precision as you can overlap the outgoing clip with the incoming clip for a nice transition between clips. It also lets you adjust the starting and ending frames of a transition between clips.

1. Double-click either the left or right border of a clip in the timeline. The Precision Editor opens. Based on whether you choose the first clip or a clip in the middle of the movie timeline, the Precision Editor displays a little differently:

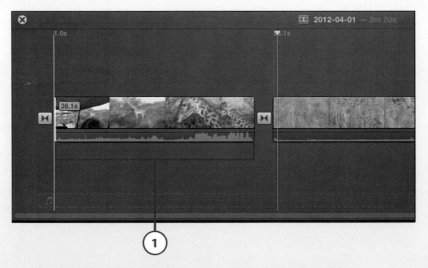

(1)

- Display of first clip in the timeline opened in the Precision Editor

**Transition
adjustment   First clip   Edit Point
tool   of movie   button**

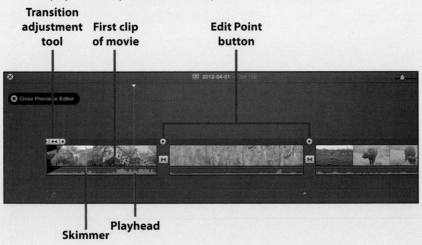

Skimmer **Playhead**

• Display of any clip other than the first clip in the movie timeline opened in the Precision Editor. In the figure, the Precision Editor displays the starting frame of the incoming clip and the ending frame of the outgoing clip in the movie project.

Outgoing   Transition   Edit point
clip   adjustment tool   button

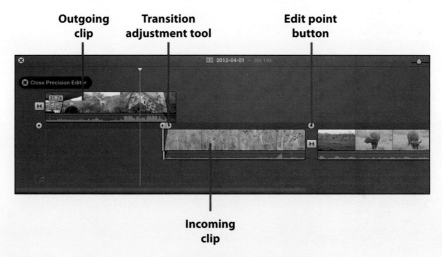

**Incoming
clip**

Use a Command to Open the Precision Editor

You can also open the Precision Editor by selecting the movie clip in the timeline and then choosing Window, Show Precision Editor.

**Show Precision
Editor command**

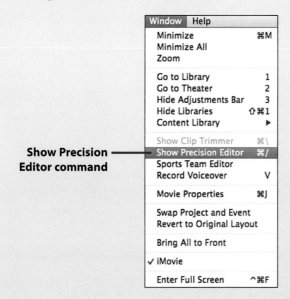

2. Even though the display is a little different based on what clip you are editing, the tools of the Precision Editor work the same. To edit the starting or ending frames of a clip, click and drag the left or right border of the active clip in the Precision Editor.

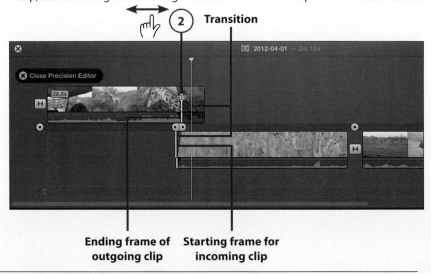

Ending frame of   Starting frame for
outgoing clip   incoming clip

Changing the Clip Duration by Dragging

Another way to lengthen or shorten a clip in the Precision Editor is to click and drag from the center of the clip, left or right. The entire clip moves and the clip is either shortened or lengthened in its duration based on the direction you drag. You need to adjust the transition duration as it becomes longer, as you make the clip duration shorter; conversely, the transition becomes shorter as you make the clip longer in duration.

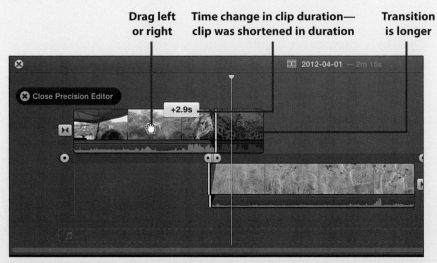

3. To change the incoming clip transition, drag the incoming clip transition start frame to the left to shorten or to the right to lengthen the transition.

4. To change the outgoing clip transition, drag the outgoing clip end frame to the right to shorten the transition or to the left to lengthen the transition.

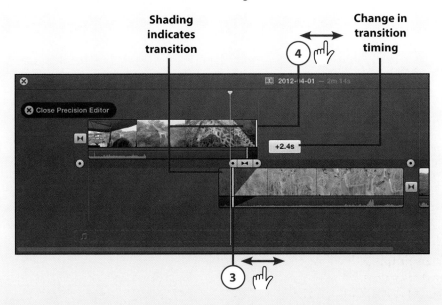

5. To modify the transition starting and ending frames in both the incoming and outgoing clip, click the Starting/Ending Frame button in the middle of the Transition Adjustment tool and drag left or right. The incoming and the outgoing transition lengthen or shorten based on the direction you drag.

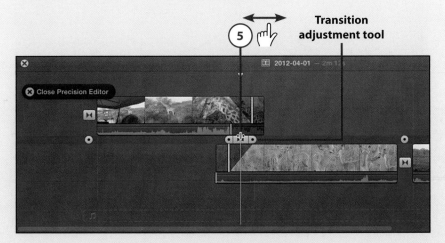

6. You can also adjust the audio track of the incoming and outgoing clips so that the audio ends or begins where you want it or overlaps between the two clips. Make sure you have your audio waveforms displayed by choosing View, Show Waveforms.

7. To adjust the audio starting and ending frames, position your mouse pointer on the audio edit point in the audio waveform, the pointer becomes the double-headed arrow. Click and drag the audio edit point left or right for either the incoming or outgoing clip.

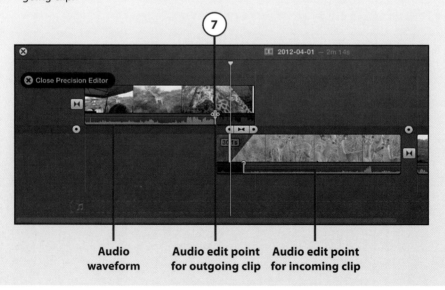

Audio waveform   Audio edit point for outgoing clip   Audio edit point for incoming clip

8. To edit different incoming and outgoing clips in your movie timeline, click a different edit point button in the Precision Editor.

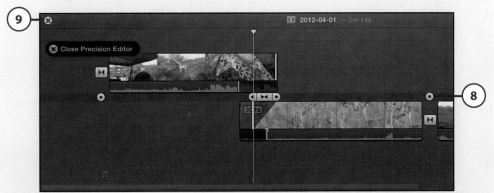

9. To close the Precision Editor, click the Close Precision Editor button or press Return on your keyboard.

Another Way to Close the Precision Editor

You can also close the Precision Editor by clicking anywhere in a blank area of the Project Browser.

Correcting a Shaky Movie

Due to the nature of handheld video cameras, sometimes you record a movie that has shaky video. iMovie has a fix for this problem by zooming in and cropping the clip to smooth out the video.

1. In the Event Browser or the movie timeline, select a clip with shaky video by clicking it.

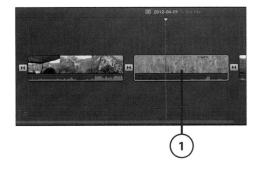

2. Click the Adjust button to display the Adjustment bar above the Viewer. You can also right-click a clip in the movie timeline and choose Adjust from the context menu.

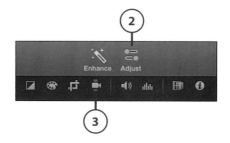

3. Click the Stabilization button to see the Stabilization options.

4. Select the Stabilize Shaky Video check box.

Understanding How iMovie Stabilizes Video

If you are stabilizing the video of a long clip, stabilization can take a long time. iMovie is actually zooming in and cropping your video so that it can focus on just the subject matter in the clip and keep it centered. This gets rid of the shaky video. The more stabilization that you apply, the more zoom and cropping iMovie applies to the clip.

5. While iMovie is stabilizing the video, an indicator shows that work is in progress. When it's finished, the Stabilize Shaky Video check box displays a check mark, and the Stabilize Shaky Video slider displays the amount of stabilization applied to the clip. You can still work with iMovie while the clip is being stabilized, though not with the clip that is being stabilized.

6. Preview the stabilized movie by moving your mouse into the Viewer, which causes the Playback options to display, and then click the Play button.

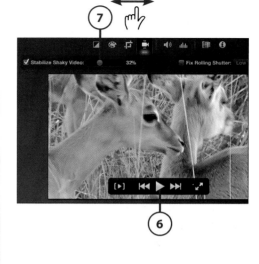

7. Adjust the Stabilize Shaky Video slider if you need more stabilization applied. The Viewer displays the clip with the new stabilization setting. The more stabilization you apply, the more iMovie zooms in on the clip and the more it crops it, enabling a smoother playback of the video.

Reverting a Stabilized Video to Original Format

After you apply stabilization to a video, you can revert the video to its original format by adjusting the Stabilize Shaky Video slider to 0% stabilization. You can also click the Remove Stabilization Adjustments button to revert the video to its original recorded state.

Stabilization set to 0%   **Remove Stabilization Adjustments button**

Correcting Blurry or Distorted Video

Another problem that can occur when you record video is blurry images caused by quick movements of the camera while recording, which is called rolling shutter distortion. iMovie can reduce this distortion with its Rolling Shutter feature.

1. In the Event Browser or the movie timeline, select a clip with blurry or distorted video by clicking it.

2. Click the Adjust button.

3. This displays the Adjustment bar above the Viewer. Click the Shaky Video button to display the Stabilization options.

4. Select the Fix Rolling Shutter check box. The Fix Rolling Shutter check box displays with a red dash indicating that iMovie is applying this adjustment to the video. Based on the length of the video, this can take some time.

5. When iMovie is done applying the Rolling Shutter adjustment, the Fix Rolling Shutter check box displays with a check mark.

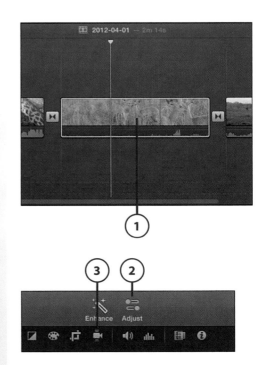

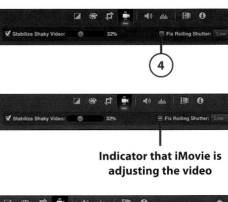

Indicator that iMovie is adjusting the video

6. Preview the adjusted movie in the Viewer by moving your mouse into the Viewer, which causes the Playback options to display, and clicking the Play button to play the movie.

⑥

7. To set the amount of Rolling Shutter adjustment to apply, click the Fix Rolling Shutter menu and choose the amount of adjustment you need. iMovie applies the new amount of Rolling Shutter adjustment to the video clip. Preview the movie in the Viewer to see the new setting applied for the Rolling Shutter adjustment.

8. If you want to remove the Rolling Shutter adjustment, click the Remove Stabilization Adjustments button.

⑦

Undoing Rolling Shutter Adjustments

You can also remove the Rolling Shutter adjustment applied to a clip by choosing Edit, Undo immediately after applying this stabilization adjustment.

⑧

Splitting Clips

Another useful feature iMovie offers is the ability to split a movie clip at any point in the video footage. This lets you take a very large movie clip and divide it into two clips. Then you can fine-tune the starting and ending frames through any of the techniques for trimming a clip covered earlier in this chapter.

1. Click and select the movie clip that you want to divide into two clips in the movie timeline.

2. Move your mouse pointer over the clip to display the skimmer, and skim through the video by moving the mouse pointer left or right. Position the skimmer at the frame in the video that you want to split the clip.

3. Click to set the playhead at that frame.

4. Right-click the clip in the movie timeline and choose Split Clip from the context menu.

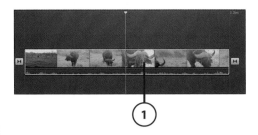

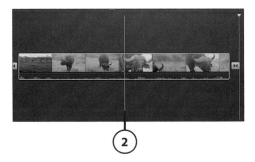

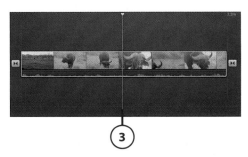

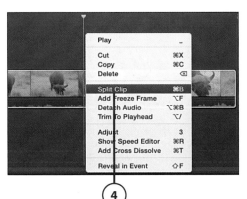

Joining Split Clips Back into One Clip

You can join the two clips created when you split a clip in the movie timeline. Select both clips in the movie timeline by shift-clicking them and selecting Modify, Join Clips.

You can also undo the split immediately after you split the clip by selecting Edit, Undo Split.

Join Clips command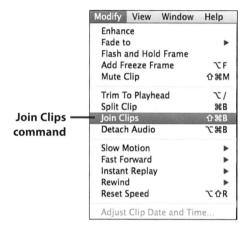

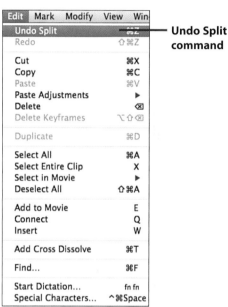 — **Undo Split command**

Merge Movie Clips

You can merge clips, but you can't do it in the movie timeline. To merge movie clips, you need to work in the Event Browser.

1. Select the movie clips you want to merge by double-clicking a clip in the Event Browser and then hold the Command key on your keyboard while you click any other clips you want to merge.

2. Select Edit, Connect. This connects the clips into one clip.

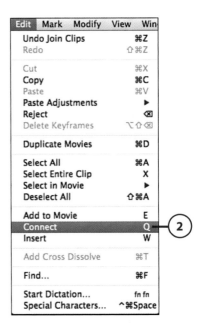

Deleting Movie Clips

If you find that a clip just does not work with your movie project, you can delete it from your movie timeline in the Project Browser.

1. Select the movie clip to delete it from the movie timeline.

2. Press the Delete key on your keyboard or right-click and choose Delete from the context menu. iMovie deletes the clip from the movie timeline, but the clip still exists in the library and event in which it is grouped.

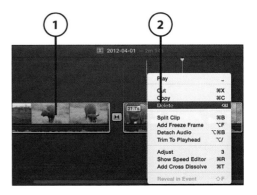

Rotating a Movie Clip

One final editing technique that can enhance a clip in your movie project is to rotate the movie clip. iMovie lets you rotate clips in their orientation by 90-degree increments.

1. Select the movie clip that you want to rotate from the movie timeline.

2. Click the Adjust button.

3. Click the Crop tool.

4. The Crop controls are displayed. You can rotate the clip clockwise by 90 degrees by clicking the Rotate the Clip Clockwise button. You can rotate the clip counterclockwise by 90 degrees by clicking the Rotate the Clip Counterclockwise button. Click multiple times to rotate the clip by 90-degree increments.

5. To apply the rotate adjustment to the movie clip, click the Apply Crop Adjustment button.

6. If you want to remove the rotate adjustment, click the Remove Crop Adjustment button.

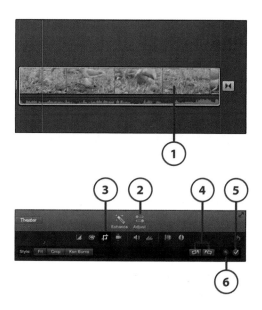

Add a title
to a movie

Speed up and
reverse a clip

Slow down a clip

In this chapter, you find out how to add special effects, maps, backgrounds, and titles to your movie clips and movie, such as how to speed up or slow down clips and add other special effects. Topics include the following:

→ Speeding up or slowing down a movie clip

→ Creating an instant replay

→ Creating the Green/Blue Screen special effect

→ Creating picture-in-picture movie clips

→ Creating side-by-side movie clips

→ Adding a map and/or background to the movie

→ Adding titles and credits to the movie and to movie clips

5

Adding Special Effects, Maps, Backgrounds, and Titles Clips

iMovie has many techniques to add special effects, maps, backgrounds, and titles to your movie clips. You can speed up or slow down a clip, as well as add the Rewind or Instant Replay special effect to a clip to add more focus or interest to the clip. You can add maps and backgrounds to your movie. Also, you can add titles to your movie and even superimpose titles over existing movie clips to add a better description of the clip and its contents. This chapter covers all of this and more!

Speeding Up or Slowing Down a Clip

iMovie can speed up or slow down a clip's playback rate. When you speed up a clip, it becomes shorter in its playback duration; when you slow down a clip, it becomes longer in its playback duration. For instance, if you double the speed of a clip, its duration is reduced by half and the clip in the timeline is displayed at one half its size.

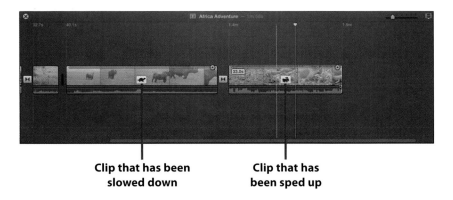

Clip that has been slowed down

Clip that has been sped up

Adjust Clip Speed

1. Select a clip in the movie timeline.

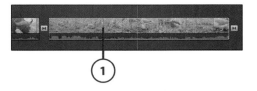

2. To slow down a clip in the movie timeline, choose Modify, Slow Motion, and then choose a speed percentage from the submenu. The Speed Editor is initiated.

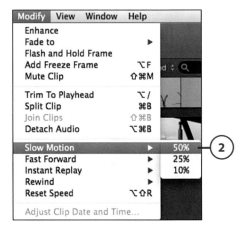

3. A turtle icon displays in the center of the clip, and the clip is lengthened in the timeline. For example, if you slow down a clip by 50%, the clip displays at double its size. The Speed slider displays at the top of the clip.

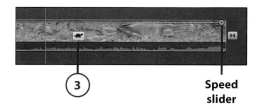

Speed slider

4. To speed up a clip in the movie timeline, choose Modify, Fast Forward, and then choose a speed option from the submenu. The Speed Editor is initiated.

5. The clip shrinks in length in the timeline, and a rabbit icon displays in the center of the clip. A Speed slider displays at the top of the clip.

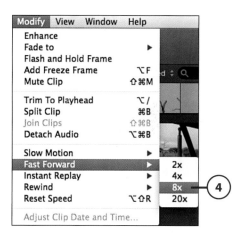

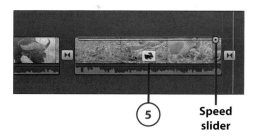

Speed slider

6. To undo a playback speed setting, select the retimed clip in the
timeline and then choose Modify,
Reset Speed.

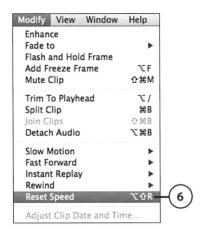

Undo Command

You can also use the Undo command to undo a speed setting
applied to a clip. Immediately
after you apply Slow Motion or
Fast Forward, choose Edit, Undo.
The Undo command will undo
any action you just initiated.

Adjust Clip Playback Speed

After you apply a playback speed like
Fast Forward or Slow Motion to a clip
in the movie timeline, you can adjust
the speed through a few different
techniques. You can manually set a
new playback speed or you can set a
custom speed setting.

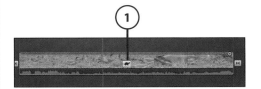

1. Select a retimed clip in the movie
timeline.

2. If the Speed Editor is not initiated,
right-click the clip and choose
Show Speed Editor from the
context menu. This is a toggle
menu—if the Speed Editor is
initiated, you will see Hide Speed
Editor in the context menu.

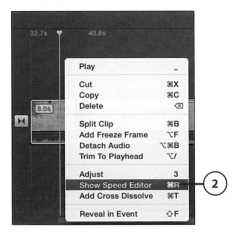

3. Click and drag the Speed slider
    left or right. Dragging left increas-
    es the speed of the clip, and
    dragging right slows down the
    clip. The new adjusted playback
    timing is displayed above the end
    of the clip, indicating the retimed
    clip duration.

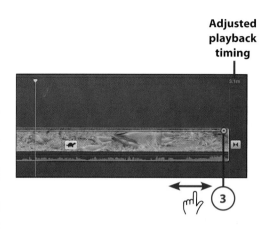

**Adjusted
playback
timing**

Using the Speed Editor
You can initiate the Speed Editor
at any time. It allows you to set
any speed you want—not just the
preset values you get with the
Modify, Slow Motion or Modify,
Fast Forward commands. Select a
clip in the movie timeline, right-
click, and then choose Show
Speed Editor from the context
menu. Adjust the Speed slider to
the speed you want.

Adding a Movie Clip with a Different Frame per Second Rate to a Movie
Recording devices record video at a default frame per second rate, or FPS, that
might be different from the iMovie default setting of 30FPS. When you import
these clips to iMovie, it automatically adjusts them to 30FPS. If you need to
retime these clips, initiate the Speed Editor and adjust the speed of these clips
by dragging the Speed slider so that the video in the clip plays faster or slower
as you need for the movie.

Set a Preset Speed

When you have a retimed clip, you can manually set a preset speed.

1. Click the rabbit or turtle icon displayed in the middle of a retimed clip. This opens the Speed settings for the retimed clip.

   You can also double-click the Speed slider to open the Speed settings.

2. Click the Preset option and then choose a preset percentage.

3. Click anywhere in the movie timeline area to close the Speed settings.

Applying a Custom Speed Setting

To apply a custom speed setting, select the Custom option and then type the percentage you want in the Percentage text field. If you need to adjust the Frame Per Second rate to iMovie's default setting of 30FPS, click the Automatic option and iMovie automatically adjusts the clip to 30FPS.

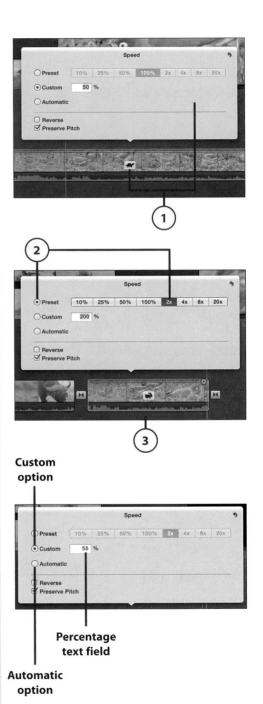

Custom option

Percentage text field

Automatic option

Adjust Audio Pitch

When you slow down or speed up a clip, you can have problems with the audio. When you slow down a clip, the audio track is also slowed down, which results in the audio having a lower pitch and sounding funny. If you speed up a clip, the audio has a higher pitch and again sounds funny. iMovie can retain the original pitch of the audio soundtrack.

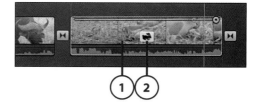

1. Click a retimed clip in the movie timeline to select it.

2. Click the turtle or rabbit indicator in the middle of the retimed clip to open the Speed settings.

3. Select the Preserve Pitch check box.

4. Click anywhere in the movie time-line area to close the Speed set-tings.

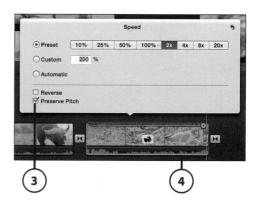

Reverse a Movie

iMovie can also reverse the direction of the video footage in a movie clip so that it plays backward. Use the Speed settings to apply this adjust-ment to your movie clip.

1. Click a retimed clip in the movie timeline to select it.

2. Click the turtle or rabbit indicator in the middle of the retimed clip to open the Speed settings.

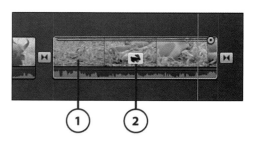

3. Select the Reverse check box.

4. Click anywhere in the movie time-line area to close the Speed settings.

Applying Multiple Speed Settings to a Clip

You can apply multiple Speed settings to a clip. For instance, you can reverse the video for a clip that has Fast Forward or Slow Motion applied to it. In the timeline, the clip displays either the rabbit or turtle indicator but flips it to the left to indicate that the clip has been reversed and retimed.

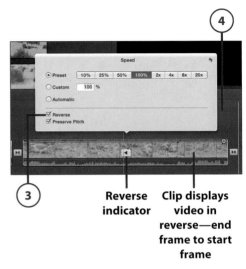

Reverse indicator   **Clip displays video in reverse—end frame to start frame**

Undoing the Speed Settings

To undo any of the Speed settings you have set for a clip, open the Speed Editor by clicking the rabbit or turtle icon in a retimed clip, and then click the Undo Speed Settings button in the upper-right corner.

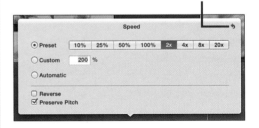

Reversed retimed clip indicator

Undo Speed Setting button

Resetting a Retimed Clip Directly in Movie Timeline

You can also reset any clip directly in the movie timeline by selecting a retimed clip and choosing Modify, Reset Speed.

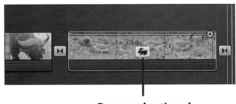

Apply the Rewind Special Effect

iMovie has a special effect that you can apply to a clip that makes it appear to rewind. The Rewind effect modifies the clip so it has three parts. The first part is where the movie plays forward; the second part is where the rewind section plays backward; and the third part is where the clip plays forward again. You can adjust each of the three parts playback speed.

1. Click a clip in the movie timeline to select it.

2. Select Modify, Rewind and then choose the rewind speed from the submenu. The submenu sets the speed of only the rewind video in part 2.

3. The Rewind special effect is applied to the clip and it displays with three parts. Each part has its own Speed slider, allowing individual adjustments for each part.

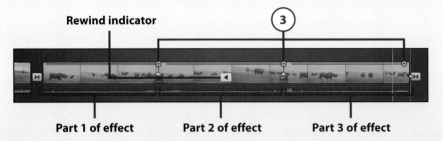

Rewind indicator

Part 1 of effect   **Part 2 of effect**   **Part 3 of effect**

4. Adjust the speed of each part by clicking the Speed slider and dragging it to the left to increase that part's playback speed. Drag to the right to slow down that part's playback speed.

5. The clip displays either the rabbit or the turtle indicator for each part of the Rewind special effect.

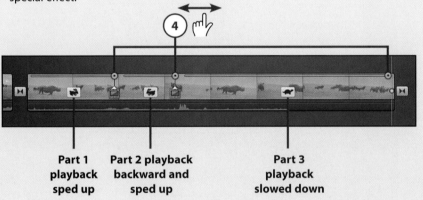

Part 1 playback sped up   **Part 2 playback backward and sped up**   **Part 3 playback slowed down**

Creating an Instant Replay of a Clip

Another effect that can provide interest to a movie clip is the Instant Replay effect. Just like in a sporting event when they cut away from the game to replay a great moment, you can create a replay of a clip.

1. Click a clip in the movie timeline to select it.

2. Choose Modify, Instant Replay and then choose the speed for the replay.

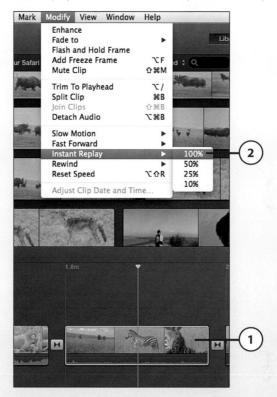

3. In the movie timeline, the selected clip displays in two segments, the clip at normal speed and the Instant Replay segment set at the speed you choose. Each segment has a Speed slider above it. Click and drag the Speed slider to adjust the speed for each segment.

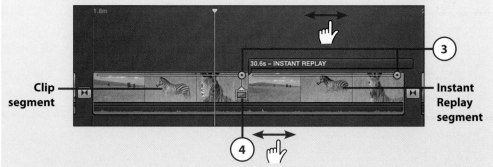

4. Click and drag the speed boundary indicator to adjust what frame to start the Instant Replay segment of the clip.

5. Double-click the Speed slider to access more Speed settings for each segment of the instant replay. If you choose a slow speed, the turtle indicator displays in the clip segment. If you choose a fast speed, the rabbit indicator displays.

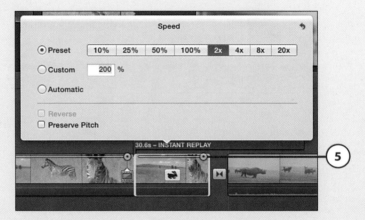

Adding Backgrounds Using the Green/Blue Screen

The Green/Blue Screen effect is a cool feature of iMovie, and it is a way to superimpose a clip on top of another clip. For instance, you might have a clip of the ocean and you want to superimpose your children walking on the beach. You need to have two clips for this effect: one that has been recorded in front of a green or blue backdrop—your children walking, in this example—and the other that is a clip you want to use as the background—in this case, the ocean. iMovie drops out the green or blue backdrop so that the first image is superimposed on the new background.

When to Use a Green Screen or a Blue Screen

iMovie's Green/Blue Screen effect drops out all blues or all greens in a clip based on the color of the backdrop you used when recording. It is wise to think about the colors used in your clip and how they contrast with the backdrop color. For example, if you are recording a green parrot, you would want to use a blue screen as it will contrast well with the green of the parrot. If your parrot is blue, you would want to use a green screen.

Add a Background

1. Place both clips in your movie timeline.

2. Click and drag the Green Screen clip above the Background clip.

3. With the Green Screen clip selected, click the Adjust button.

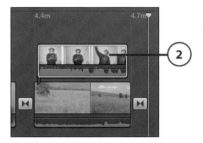

Background clip   **Green Screen clip**   (1)

Access Adjust Button with a Right-Click

You can right-click on any clip in the movie timeline and choose Adjust from the Context menu to initiate the clip adjustment tools.

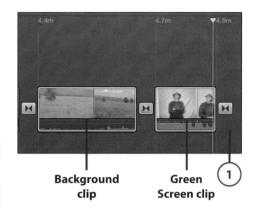

4. Click the Video Overlay Settings button.

5. Click the Video Overlay button and select Green/Blue Screen from the drop-down menu.

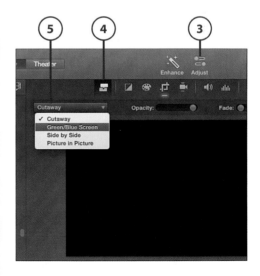

6. The Viewer displays the Green Screen clip superimposed over the Background clip.

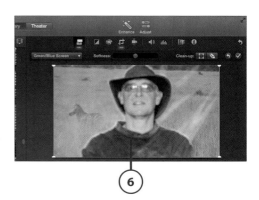

6

USING A BACKGROUND IMAGE WITH THE GREEN/BLUE SCREEN EFFECT

>>>Go Further

You can add a background image to your movie and then place the super-imposed image on the background. iMovie has a library for maps and back-grounds. In the sidebar is the Content Library, which contains the Maps & Backgrounds Library. The Event Browser displays all the maps and back-grounds and, just like with a movie clip, you can just click and drag a back-ground image to the movie timeline. Then you can create the Green/Blue Screen effect on top of the Background clip. See "Add a Background" task later in this chapter for how to add a background to your movie project.

Green/ Blue Screen effect

Maps & Backgrounds Library

Background from Content Library

Make Green Screen Adjustments

It is common to need to apply a few adjustments to your Green/Blue Screen clip to help clear up issues that display when iMovie drops the backdrop out of the clip. Sample issues include the tightness of the cropping edges to the subject matter or folds and creases in the backdrop that still are visible even though the backdrop was dropped out of the clip.

1. Click to select the clip with a Green/Blue Screen effect. This displays the Green/Blue Screen toolbar.

2. Click and drag the Edge Softness slider to adjust the softness of the edges around your subject of the Green/Blue Screen clip.

3. Click the Crop button and in the Viewer, click and drag the cropping handles to adjust the size of the Green/Blue Screen effect.

4. To fix problem areas, click the Clean-up button and drag across areas that need more Green/Blue Screen effect applied.

5. To revert the clip to its original state, click the Reset Video Overlay Settings button.

6. When you have adjusted the Green/Blue Screen effect the way you want, click the Apply Green/Blue Screen Settings button to finalize your adjustments.

Cropping edge   **Folds in backdrop**

Green/Blue Screen toolbar

Viewer displaying Green/Blue Screen effect

Adjusted Green/Blue Screen area

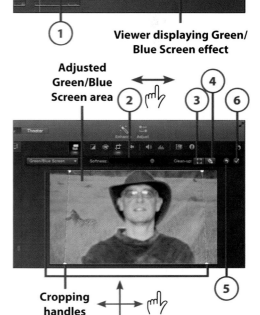

Cropping handles

Beware of Cropping the Green/Blue Screen Area Too Small

Always preview the cropping that you set for your Green/Blue Screen effect as you might find that you set the cropping area too small. Based on the movement of your subject in the clip, it might require a larger area to show your subject throughout each frame of the clip's video.

Using Picture-in-Picture

iMovie lets you create a video effect that displays a second window of a clip inside another clip. This is called the picture-in-picture effect.

Picture-in-picture

Apply the Picture-in-Picture Effect

1. Click and drag the clip that you want to be in the smaller window above a clip in the movie timeline.

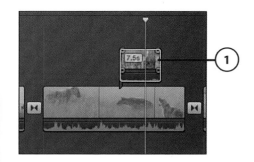

Moving the Picture-in-Picture Window

You can adjust the location of the picture-in-picture window in the main clip video by dragging it left or right above the main clip in the movie timeline.

You can also adjust the size of the picture-in-picture window by clicking and dragging the corner handles of the window that display on the window in the Viewer.

Resize arrow tool   **Resize handles**

Location indicator for positioning window clip at exact frame in the main clip

2. Click the Adjust button in the iMovie toolbar.

3. Click the Video Overlay Settings button.

4. Choose Picture in Picture from the Choose a Video Overlay Style menu.

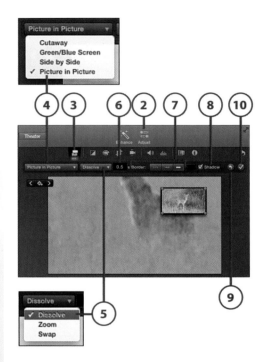

5. Set the transition of how the second clip window enters and exits the movie by clicking the Choose Transition Style menu and selecting the transition that you want for the window. To display the Window clip with a transition of dissolve or zoom, choose Dissolve or Zoom. Choose Swap to switch locations of the main clip and the window clip, with the main clip becoming the picture window and the picture window clip becoming the background

6. Double-click the transition duration and then delete the default transition time of 0.5 seconds; type in the transition duration that you want.

7. Click one of the three border settings to apply a border to your window.

8. Click the Shadow option. This applies a shadow to your window.

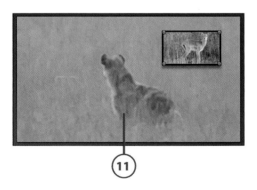

9. Click the Reset Video Overlay Settings button to revert the clip to its original settings.

10. When you have the picture-in-picture settings the way you want, click the Apply Picture in Picture Settings button to finalize your settings.

11. The Viewer displays the movie with the picture-in-picture effect applied.

Creating Side by Side Clips

Similar to the picture-in-picture clip, you can create two clips that play side-by-side at the same time. This splits the screen to display both clips at the same time.

Side-by-side overlay

Display Side-by-Side Clips

1. Drag a clip or a portion of a clip above a clip in the movie timeline.

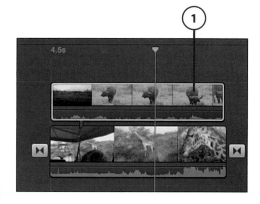

2. Click the Adjust button in the iMovie toolbar.

3. Click the Video Overlay Settings button.

4. Choose Side by Side from the Choose a Video Overlay Style menu.

5. Click either the Left or Right button to rearrange which side the side-by-side clips display.

6. Click and drag the Slide In/Slide Out transition to set a transition duration for the side-by-side clips.

7. Manually set a transition duration by double-clicking the Transition Duration Setting text box. Delete the duration setting in the text box and type in the duration you want.

8. Click the Reset Video Overlay Settings button to revert the clip to its original settings.

9. Click the Apply Side-by-Side Settings button to finalize your settings.

10. The Viewer displays the movie with the side-by-side effect applied.

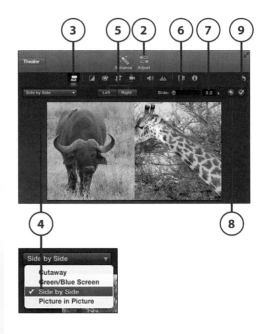

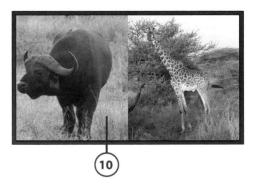

Adding Maps & Backgrounds to a Movie

You can add maps and background images to your movie. iMovie has a Content Library loaded with extras for making your movie more detailed or descriptive. The Content Library is in the iMovie sidebar, and the Maps & Backgrounds Library is in the Content Library. Each map style has a short animation of the route taken from your starting location to your ending location. You can configure any city, state, or country as the starting and ending location and customize the map style. And you have a choice of backgrounds, both patterned or solid styles, and some have animation for the display.

Add an Interactive Map

1. Click the Maps & Backgrounds Library in the Content Library.

2. Select a map style in the Event Browser. Skim through the map style by moving your mouse pointer left or right to see the animation.

3. Drag the map style from the Event Browser into the movie timeline. The Viewer displays the map style.

4. Move your mouse into the Viewer to display the playback controls, and click the Play button to see the map animation.

5. You can set the route by clicking the Set Start Location menu. You can also click the Set End Location button to set end destination.

6. The Location Search window displays for setting the Start Location. Type a city, state, airport code, or just a country into the Search field. The search results display any matches.

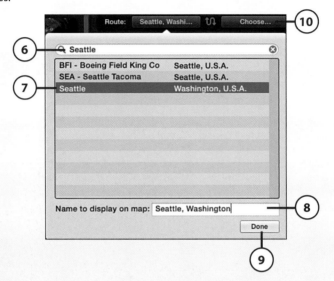

7. Click to select the city, state, airport, or country in the search results.

8. Click the Name to Display on Map field and type a name.

9. Click the Done button when you are finished with the Start Location search.

10. To create the end location, click the End Location button and repeat steps 6–9 for the End Location.

11. To set a style for the display of the location information on the map, click the Style button and select a new style from the list.

Add a Background

1. Click the Maps & Backgrounds Library in the Content Library.

Maps & Backgrounds Library   **Vertical scrollbar**

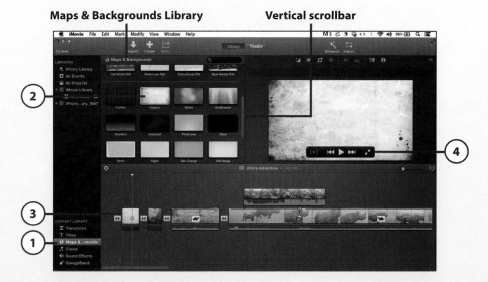

2. Select a background style in the Event Browser. Use the vertical scrollbar to scroll down to see all backgrounds.

3. Drag the background style from the Event Browser into the movie timeline. The Viewer displays the background image.

4. Move your mouse into the Viewer to display the playback controls and click the Play button to see the background animation.

5. If needed, adjust the background screen clip duration by clicking and dragging the starting and/or ending frame of the clip to the left or right.

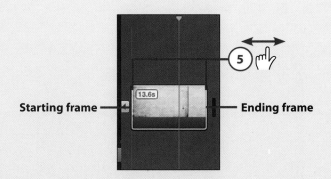

Starting frame   **Ending frame**

Adding Titles to a Movie

iMovie lets you add titles to your movie or anywhere in a clip. iMovie has 16 new title styles available. Many of these title styles have animation that displays the title in an entertaining fashion. You can add a title to any movie clip in your movie timeline. You can also use them as their own clip and add them as a title screen to the start or the end of your movie, as well as between any clips in the timeline. Movie titles are in the Content Library.

Display of title

1. Click the Titles Library listed in the Content Library.
2. Click to select a title style from the Event Browser.
3. Drag the selected title style from the Event Browser and drop it in the movie timeline before or after a movie clip.

Searching for a Title Style

You can also search for a title style by name in the Search field above the Event Browser.

Search field

4. The Viewer displays the title screen. Double-click the title field shown in the Viewer to set your cursor in a title line and then click and drag over the default title text to select it.

Quick Access to Title Screen in Viewer

Another technique for selecting the default title text in a title screen is to double-click the purple title screen clip in the movie timeline. This automatically displays the title screen clip in the Viewer with the first default text field already selected.

5. Delete the default text by pressing Delete on the keyboard, and type in the title you want for your title screen.

Adjusting Title Screen Clip Duration

When a title screen is created in the timeline, it displays as a purple clip with a default duration setting. You can extend or shorten the title screen clip by dragging the right or left borders of the clip just like you can for extending or shortening the duration of any clip in the movie timeline.

Add Title Text to Movie Clips

You can also add title text to any clip in your movie timeline. This enables you to add comments or titles directly in your movie clips. The process is similar to adding a title screen to your movie but instead of placing the title style in the movie timeline as its own clip, you add it above a clip in the timeline as an overlay clip. The title and its animation are superimposed on the existing clip in the movie timeline.

Title style as overlay clip

1. Click the Titles Library in the Content Library.

2. Click to select a title style from the Event Browser.

3. Drag the title style and place it over an existing clip in the movie timeline.

Positioning the Title Style
Position the title style over the center of a clip in the Movie timeline to display the title throughout all the video of the clip. If you position the title style in the opening third or ending third of the clip, iMovie displays the title for the video of just that third of the clip.

4. The Viewer displays the clip with the title style superimposed over it. Double-click the default title text to select it and press Delete on your keyboard to delete the default text.

5. Type the text you want to be displayed on the existing movie clip.

Some Titles Styles Cannot Be a Title Screen

There are also some titles styles that can only be added to an existing clip in the movie—Lens Flare and Pull Focus. They cannot be added as a title screen; they can only be added as a title style superimposed over an existing clip in the movie timeline.

Adding a Titles Style to a Background Screen Clip

You can also create a title screen using a background style as the background image. First add a background style from the Maps & Backgrounds Library in the Content Library to the movie timeline. Then overlay a title style above the background screen clip in the movie timeline.

Customize Title Font Properties

After you have the titles added to your movie, you can customize the font properties, like the font used or the font size, alignment, and color. Based on the title style used in your movie, some or all font properties might not be accessible. Each title style has its own customizable font properties.

1. Click to select a title screen clip or overlay title clip in your movie timeline.

2. Double-click the title text in the Viewer and select all the text by dragging over it.

3. The Titles toolbar displays above the Viewer. The tools displayed vary based on the selected title style and the available font properties that can be modified for that title style.

4. Format the font by clicking the Font button and selecting a new font from the list.

5. Set a larger or smaller font size by either clicking the Font Size arrow button and selecting a preset size from the list, or by double-clicking the Font Size field and typing a custom font size.

6. Click one of the font alignment buttons to select an alignment style of either left, center, right, or fully justified.

7. Click one of the font style buttons to select a font style of Bold, Italic, or Outline.

8. Click the Font Color button and then click to select a color from the color palette.

9. If you need to reset your title style to its default settings, click the Reset Title Style button.

10. When you have all your font properties set as you want, click the Apply Title Adjustments button to finalize your font properties.

Title Styles and Customizable Font Properties

Some title styles are not customizable in their font, font size, alignment, or font color. The Titles library has 48 different title styles. The first 16 are noncustomizable in font properties, but the remaining 32 are customizable to some extent, if not fully customizable.

Using the Color Palette

The color palette is a common feature of many Apple products. It lets you choose from millions of colors. You can use the Color Wheel, which is the default color palette that displays, or if you click one of the color selection buttons, like Color Sliders, the color palette changes to a different palette for choosing a color. Click the Close button to close the color palette.

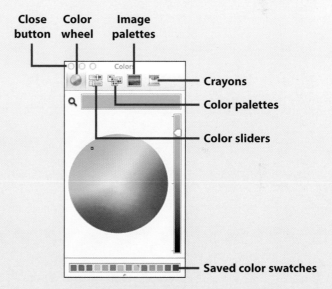

Close button   **Color wheel**   **Image palettes**

Crayons

Color palettes

Color sliders

Saved color swatches

Adding Credits at the End of Your Movie

A common practice in any movie is to add credits to your movie. The credits can be placed anywhere in the movie timeline, but typically they are located at the very end of the movie. iMovie makes this easy with a title style just for credits, the Scrolling Credits style.

Viewer displaying Scrolling Credits title style

Playhead

1. Click the Titles library in the Content Library located in the iMovie sidebar.

2. Select the Scrolling Credits title style in the Event Browser.

3. To place the Scrolling Credits title style at the end of the movie, click and drag the horizontal scrollbar to the right so that you can see the end of your movie timeline.

4. Click and drag the Scrolling Credits title style to the end of your movie to place it after the last movie clip.

5. To customize the credits displayed, move the playhead into the Scrolling Credits title screen in the timeline to display the credits in the Viewer. Then double-click the default text in the Title field to select all the text.

6. Press Delete on your keyboard to delete the default text and type in the new title text.

7. Repeat steps 5 and 6 to replace the other credits' default text fields. If there are more default title fields than what you need, click and drag through them to select the extras and press Delete on your keyboard to delete them.

8. Add more text fields by putting your cursor at the end of a credit text field and pressing Return on your keyboard to create a new line.

9. Press Tab on your keyboard to move to the left-center text field and type the text you want.

10. Press Tab again to move to the right-center text field and type the text you want.

Adjusting the Clip Duration

You can adjust the duration of the Scrolling Credits title screen by shortening or lengthening the title screen clip. Click and drag the left or right border of the clip in the movie timeline to adjust the duration of the Scrolling Credits clip.

Record a voiceover

In this chapter, you find out how to add voiceovers, music, and sound effects to movie projects. Topics include the following:

→ Adding a voiceover
→ Adding music from iTunes
→ Adding sound effects
→ Adding audio from GarageBand
→ Editing audio
→ Slowing down or speeding up audio

Adding and Editing Voiceovers, Music, and Sound Effects

A movie is nothing without some music, sound effects, and maybe a voiceover. iMovie enables you to add all three of these to your movies and also to edit the audio to get it sounding just the way you need it to.

Recording a Voiceover

A voiceover is a voice track, such as when you narrate or explain what the viewer is seeing in your movie. iMovie lets you record your voiceover directly over your movie while it's playing.

1. Click to move the playhead to approximately where you want to add your voiceover.

2. Click the View menu.

3. Click Record Voiceover. The Voiceover icons appear under your video in the Viewer.

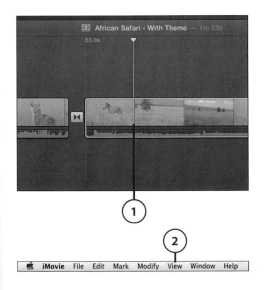

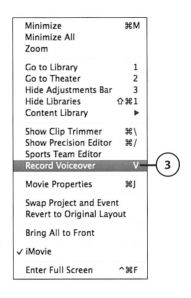

4. Click to display the Voiceover recording options.

5. Click the Input Source drop-down list to change the microphone you want to use, if neccessary.

6. Drag the Volume slider to adjust the volume of your voiceover.

7. Uncheck the Mute Project check box to unmute the original audio while you record your voiceover, or leave it checked to keep the audio muted.

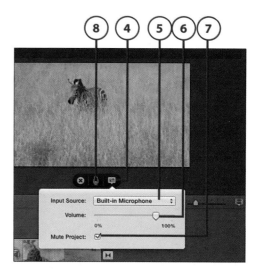

Why Would I Unmute the Audio?

In step 7 we see that we can choose to unmute the original project audio while we record our voiceover. By default, the option is selected so that the original audio is muted. Otherwise, while you are recording your voiceover, it could be distracting if the original audio from the project continues to play as you speak. However, if you feel that you need to hear the original audio as you speak, simply uncheck the box.

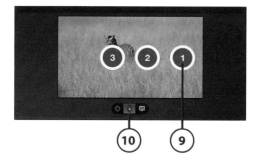

8. Click the Microphone icon to start recording your voiceover. The icon turns red while the recording is in process.

9. Wait for the countdown to reach 1, and then begin speaking.

10. Click the Microphone icon to stop recording the voiceover.

Adding Music from iTunes

You can add music you have stored in your iTunes library to your movie to enhance the mood.

1. Click iTunes in the Content Library.

2. Click to filter the list of content in iTunes to specific categories, such as Podcasts, Music, or TV Shows, and to select specific playlists.

3. Click in the Search field and type a search term to quickly find the audio you are looking for.

4. Double-click a song to start playing it.

5. Drag the song to the music placeholder in the timeline.

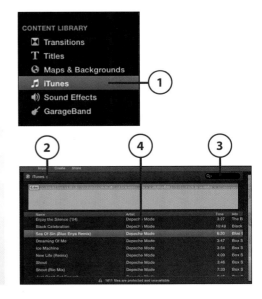

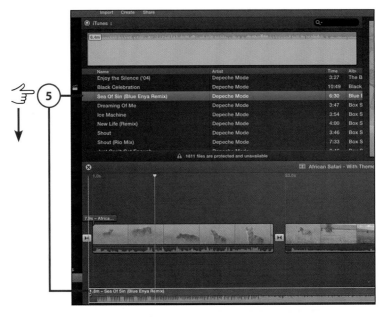

Adding Sound Effects

iMovie comes preloaded with many sound effects and theme music that you can use in your movies.

1. Click Sound Effects in the Content Library.

2. Click to filter the list of content to specific categories, such as jingles, machines, people, or theme music.

3. Click in the Search field and type a search term to quickly find the sound effect you are looking for.

4. Double-click a sound effect to start playing it.

5. Drag the sound effect to above or below your timeline.

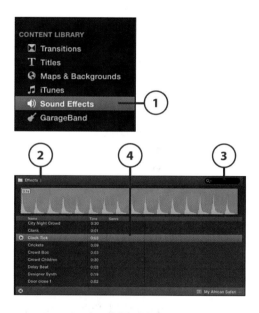

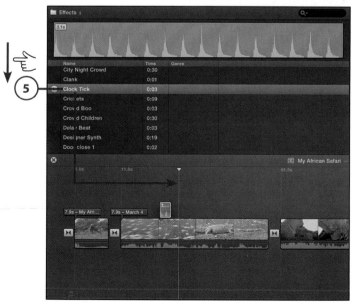

Adding Audio from GarageBand

If you have some audio you have put together in GarageBand, you can add it to your movie.

1. Click GarageBand in the Content Library.

2. Click to filter the list of content if you use folders when saving your GarageBand files.

3. Click in the Search field and type a search term to quickly find a GarageBand project.

4. Double-click a GarageBand project to start playing it.

5. Drag the GarageBand project to above or below your timeline.

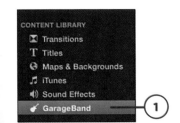

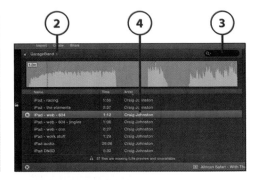

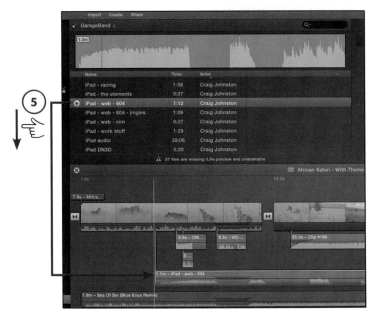

Editing Audio

Regardless of whether you've used a voiceover, iTunes music, sound effects, or a GarageBand project, you can edit the way your audio sounds, including adding fade-in and fade-out.

1. Drag the horizontal black line up and down to increase or reduce the level of the audio.

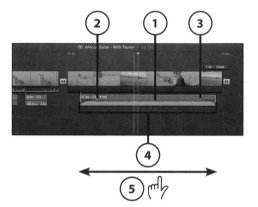

2. Drag the slider to the left or right to decrease or increase the amount of time it takes to fade in the audio. Moving the slider all the way to the left means the audio starts instantly with no fade-in.

3. Drag the slider to the left or right to increase or decrease the amount of time it takes to fade out the audio. Moving the slider all the way to the right means the audio ends instantly with no fade-out.

4. Drag the outer edges of the audio to lengthen or shorten it.

5. Drag the audio left and right to reposition it.

Slowing Down or Speeding Up Audio

You can also slow down or speed up the audio as needed.

1. Right-click an audio clip and choose Show Speed Editor.

2. Drag the Clip speed slider to the left or right to slow down or speed up the audio.

3. Click the speed adjustment line for a more accurate and flexible way of audio speed adjustment.

4. Choose one of the Preset audio speeds by clicking the speed you desire.

5. Click Custom and enter a custom audio speed in the text field.

6. Click the Reverse check box to make the audio play in reverse.

7. Click the Preserve Pitch check box to preserve the pitch of the audio when it is being played in reverse, or when the clip has been sped up or slowed down.

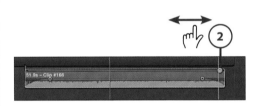

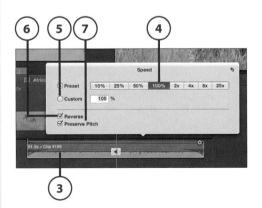

>>>Go Further

CAN I EDIT THE AUDIO IN MY ORIGINAL VIDEO?

This section has discussed how to edit the audio you have added to your project, such as a voiceover, music from iTunes, and so on, but what about the audio that is in your original video? Can you have the same kind of control over that audio? The answer is yes. You need to detach the audio from the video, and then you can edit it on its own. To do this, select the video clip you want to detach the audio from. Right-click and choose Detach Audio. After the audio has been detached from its original video footage, you can use all the methods described in this section to edit it.

Play	␣
Cut	⌘X
Copy	⌘C
Delete	⌫
Split Clip	⌘B
Add Freeze Frame	⌥F
Detach Audio	⌥⌘B
Trim To Playhead	⌥/
Adjust	3
Show Speed Editor	⌘R
Add Cross Dissolve	⌘T
Reveal in Event	⇧F

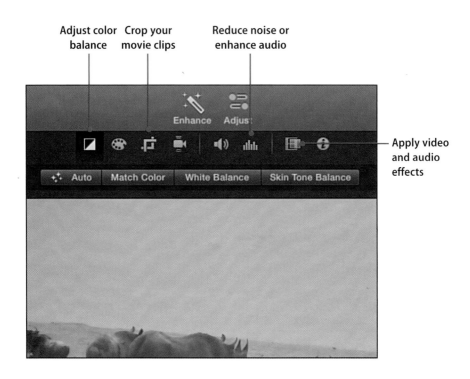

Adjust color balance

Crop your movie clips

Reduce noise or enhance audio

Apply video and audio effects

Enhance   Adjust

Auto   Match Color   White Balance   Skin Tone Balance

In this chapter, you find out how to make adjustments to your movie clips to make them look and sound better. Topics include the following:

→ Letting iMovie automatically enhance your movie clips
→ Adjusting color balance, brightness, temperature, and saturation
→ Fixing rolling shutter and stabilizing shaky video
→ Adjusting movie clip volume and overall sound

Editing Video Color, Brightness, and More

When you import movie clips into iMovie, unless you are an expert videographer the clips will likely need some attention to make them look and sound better. You might even need to stabilize shaky video. Luckily, iMovie has all the tools to turn your amateur video into a professional movie.

Using the Adjust Menu

Before you can make any adjustments to your video, you first must show the Adjust menu.

1. Click on a movie clip or select part of a clip.

2. Click Adjust. The Adjust menu opens.

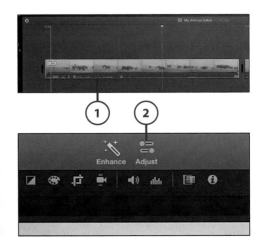

Adjusting Color Balance

If you need to adjust the color balance, or intensities of colors, globally across a movie clip, you can use the Color Balance menu.

1. Click the Color Balance icon.

2. Click Auto to allow iMovie to automatically enhance the movie clip for you.

3. Click Match Color to match the color in the movie clip with the color in another movie clip. Follow the steps in the "Match Color" section later in this chapter.

4. Click White Balance to adjust the color in the movie clip based on a part of the clip that you know is white or gray. Follow the steps in the "Adjust White Balance" section later in this chapter.

5. Click Skin Tone Balance to adjust the colors in the movie clip based on human skin tone of someone in the clip. Follow the steps in the "Adjust Skin Tone" section later in this chapter.

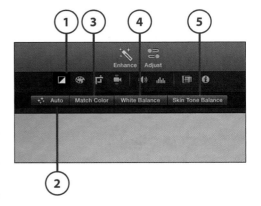

Letting iMovie Decide

If you don't feel like experimenting with adjusting the color balance in your movie clip, you can let iMovie take a stab at it. Just click Auto and iMovie analyzes the clip and makes global color adjustments to it to make it appear as natural as possible.

Match Color

1. Skim through your movie clips by hovering your cursor over the frames. The cursor looks like an eyedropper.

2. Click a frame to preview how your movie clip will look using the colors from the frame you have clicked on.

3. Click the check mark to save your changes.

Frame you clicked on

Preview of your clip with adjusted colors ③

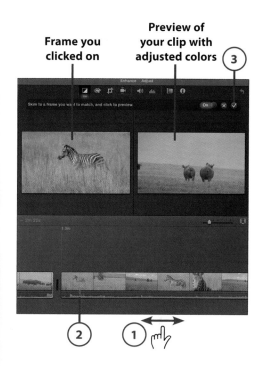

② ① ✋

Adjust White Balance

To use the White Balance feature, make sure you are viewing a frame within your movie clip that has white or gray in it.

1. Click an area in the frame that is white or gray, such as a cloud or a white wall.

2. Look at the preview to see if you like how the color has been adjusted.

3. Click the check mark to save your changes.

① ③

Adjust Skin Tone

To use the Skin Tone Balance feature, make sure you are viewing a frame within your movie clip that has a person in it so you can use his or her skin tone.

1. Click the face or body of someone in the frame.

2. Look at the preview to see if you like how the color has been adjusted, and if the skin tones look natural.

3. Click the check mark to save your changes.

Correcting Color

If you need to correct the colors in a movie clip, you can use the Color Correction menu to adjust contrast, brightness, color saturation, and color temperature.

1. Click the Color Correction icon.

2. Slide to adjust shadows in the clip to be lighter or darker.

3. Slide to adjust the contrast between light and dark colors in the clip.

4. Slide to adjust the overall brightness of the clip.

5. Slide to adjust the highlights in the clip to make them brighter or darker.

6. Slide to adjust the overall color saturation of the clip.

7. Slide to adjust the overall color temperature of the clip to be cooler or warmer.

Click to undo your changes

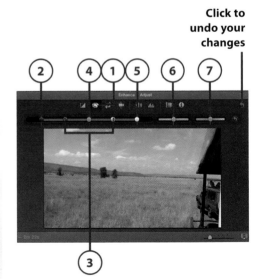

Cropping

If you need to crop your movie clip to show only part of the frames, rotate the clips, or use a Ken Burns effect, you can use the Cropping menu.

View the Cropping Menu

1. Click the Cropping icon.

2. Click to make your clip fill the entire frame. This is the default for all clips.

3. Click to select which part of the frames in the clip are displayed.

4. Click to use a Ken Burns effect on your clip, effectively creating a postproduction zoom and pan.

5. Click to rotate the clip counter-clockwise.

6. Click to rotate the clip clockwise.

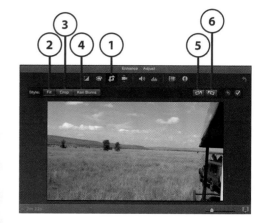

Crop

You can crop your movie clip so that only a section of the frame is displayed. This effectively zooms into a specific section.

1. Click Crop.

2. Drag the selection box by its corners to adjust what part of the frame the viewer will see.

3. Click the check mark to save your changes.

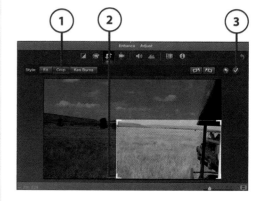

Use the Ken Burns Effect

The Ken Burns effect enables you to gradually move what the viewer sees from one area of the image to another. Think of this as a virtual camera.

1. Click the Ken Burns button.

2. Click the Start selection box and drag it around if you need to.

3. Drag the Start selection box by its corners to adjust what part of the frame the viewer will see. In this example, we made the Start area smaller than it originally was and dragged it to the top left of the frame.

4. Click the End selection box and drag it around if you need to.

5. Drag the End selection box by its corners to adjust what part of the frame the viewer will see. In this example, we made the End box smaller than it originally was and dragged it to the bottom right of the frame.

6. Click the check mark to save your changes.

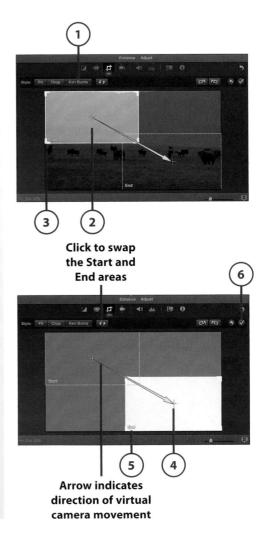

Click to swap the Start and End areas

Arrow indicates direction of virtual camera movement

Correcting for Stability and Rolling Shutter

If your movie clip is shaky, you can let iMovie stabilize the clip so that it looks like it was recorded with a steady hand. If your camera uses a rolling shutter, fast-moving or vibrating footage, objects can appear misshapen. You can use iMovie to correct that footage.

What Is Rolling Shutter?

Rolling shutter is a technique used by many digital cameras when you use them to record video. This includes many point-and-shoot cameras, Digital Single Lens Reflex (DSLR) cameras, and smartphones like the iPhone. Most of the time, you will not see the effects of rolling shutter, but in certain instances, like when images are moving very fast, the way the scene is captured on video appears to wobble or the objects appear misshapen. iMovie allows you to correct for the aftereffects of rolling shutter. You can read much more about rolling shutter at www.diyphotography.net/everything-you-wanted-to-know-about-rolling-shutter.

1. Click the Stabilization icon.

2. Click to turn on stabilization.

3. Slide to select the amount of stabilization to use.

4. Click to fix the effects that might be caused by rolling shutter.

5. Click to choose the amount of rolling shutter correction to use.

Click to undo your changes

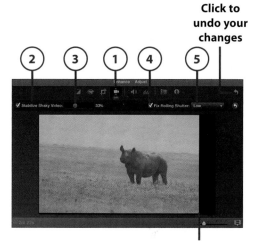

The edges of the original frames may become visible

Adjusting Volume

You can adjust the overall volume of your movie clip, or, if you have two audio clips associated with your movie clip (such as a voiceover or background music), you can reduce the volume of one of them.

1. Click the Volume icon.

2. Click to let iMovie automatically adjust the loudness of the volume in the movie clip.

3. Click to mute or unmute the audio in the clip.

4. Slide to adjust the loudness of the volume in the clip.

5. Click to reduce the volume of the unselected movie clip or extra audio clip so that it is softer than the audio in the other associated clips.

6. Slide to increase or decrease how soft the audio in the other clips must be adjusted to.

Click to undo your changes

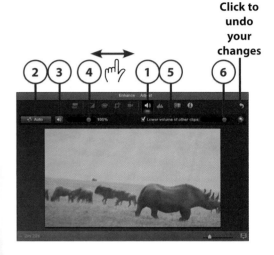

How Do I Use Lower Volume?

Let's say you have added some background music to your project. It appears as a second audio track. If you want the background music to be softer than the audio in the main movie clip, you would select your movie clip, and use the Lower Volume feature described in steps 5 and 6 to lower the volume of all other audio clips, other than the audio in the movie clip itself. The reverse can be done, too. For example, if you record a voiceover for part of your movie clip, you would want the audio in the movie clip to be softer so viewers can hear the voiceover. In this example, you would select the voiceover audio clip and use steps 5 and 6 to lower the volume of the unselected audio clips (which include the audio in your movie clip).

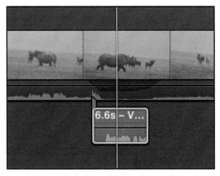

The volume of the audio in the video clip has been lowered in favor of the background music.

Using Noise Reduction and Equalizer Settings

If you need to adjust the audio in your movie clip so that the background noise is reduced or want to enhance the audio using preset equalizer settings, you can use the Noise Reduction and Equalizer settings.

1. Click the Noise Reduction and Equalizer icon.

2. Click to turn on background noise reduction.

3. Slide to choose the percentage of background noise reduction.

4. Click to choose a preset equalizer setting such as Voice Enhance, Music Enhance, Hum Reduction, Bass Boost, and so on.

Click to undo your changes

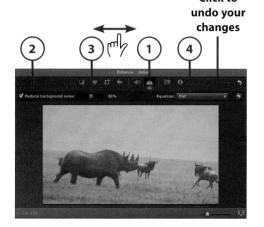

Using Video and Audio Effects

You can apply cool video and audio effects to your movie clip to change the way the clip looks and sounds.

1. Click the Video and Audio Effects icon.

2. Click to open the Choose Video Effect dialog box.

Click to undo your changes

3. Hover your cursor over a video effect to see a preview of it.

4. Click a video effect to select it and use it.

5. Click to open the Choose Audio Effect dialog box.

6. Hover your cursor over an audio effect to hear what it will sound like.

7. Click an audio effect to select it and use it.

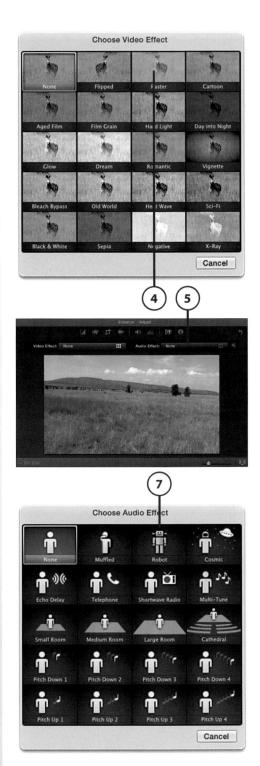

>>>Go Further

COPYING YOUR ADJUSTMENTS TO ANOTHER CLIP

After you have made adjustments to one movie clip, or part of a movie clip, you don't need to repeat them again for other clips. To copy some or all of the adjustments to a new clip, select the clip that you have already adjusted. Select Edit, Copy (or press Command+C). Then select the clip you want to copy the adjustments to. Select Edit, Paste Adjustments. When the Paste Adjustments menu appears, choose all adjustments or just ones you want to copy.

All	
Color	⌥⌘C
Crop	⌥⌘R
Stabilization	⌥⌘Z
Rolling Shutter	⌥⌘T
Volume	⌥⌘A
Video Effect	⌥⌘L
Audio Effect	⌥⌘O
Speed	⌥⌘S
Cutaway Settings	⌥⌘U
Map Style	⌥⌘M

List of adjustments that can be copied from one clip to another

Give your video a theme

THEMES

Modern
Modern

NEON
Neon

News
News

NEWSCAST
Newscast

Photo Album

Playful

Cancel   Change

In this chapter, you find out how to add video themes that automatically turn your movies into professional-looking productions. Topics include the following:

➜ Adding a video theme
➜ Adjusting the video theme

Adding and Customizing Video Themes

Video themes are predefined transitions, text treatments, and opening and ending titles that iMovie uses to enhance your video.

Creating a New Project with a Video Theme

If you are creating a new project, you can choose which theme to use at creation time.

1. Click Create.

2. Click Movie.

3. Scroll up and down to see all video themes.

4. Click a video theme to select it.

5. Click Create.

6. Type the name of your project.

7. Select the event that your project must use for source video.

8. Click OK to create your new project using the video theme you chose.

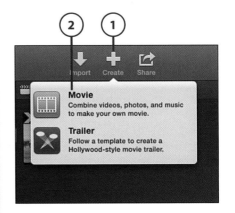

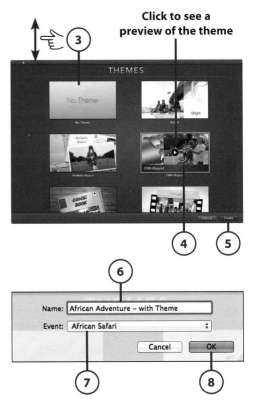

Click to see a preview of the theme

What Does the Theme Do?

If you create a new project using a video theme, iMovie automatically adds transitions and opening and ending titles. Video themes also normally have a second style of title that can be used anywhere in the middle of your movie. As you drag new video clips into your project, iMovie automatically adds a transition between the clips. At the beginning and end of your project timeline, iMovie has placed an opening and ending title to your project.

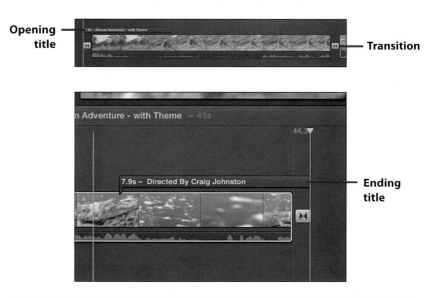

Adding a Video Theme to an Existing Project

You might have an existing project you have been working on and later decide to add a video theme to it. Use these same steps to change the theme for a project.

1. Click Settings.

2. Click No Theme to see a list of themes.

3. Scroll up and down to see all video themes.

4. Click a video theme to select it.

5. Click Change.

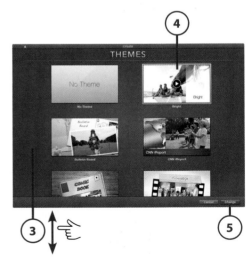

6. Click Automatic Content if it is not already checked. This feature tells iMovie to automatically add transitions and titles to your movie based on the theme you choose.

Change the Theme Titles

If necessary, you can change the text that iMovie has automatically chosen for the titles.

1. Double-click the title you want to edit.

2. Type a new title or edit the current text.

3. Click the check mark to save your changes.

Click to undo your changes

Title Styles and Customizable Font Properties

Some title styles are not customizable in their font, font size, alignment, or font color. The Titles library has 48 different title styles. The first 16 are noncustomizable in font properties, but the remaining 32 are customizable to some extent, if not fully customizable.

Add a Location

Some video themes include a map so you can tell iMovie where you recorded your video when you edit the title. iMovie shows where you were on the map during the title sequence.

1. Double-click the title you want to edit.

2. Search for a city, airport, country, or place (such as a landmark or a city name).

3. Click to select the city or place.

4. Click Done.

5. Click the check mark to save your changes.

Click to undo your changes

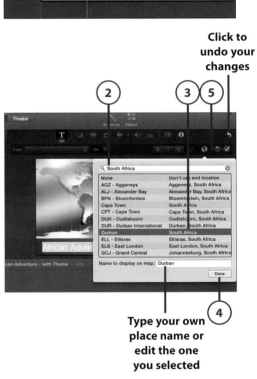

Type your own place name or edit the one you selected

Change the Transition

When you choose a video theme, iMovie uses a predefined transition between clips. You can choose a different transition on a case-by-case basis.

1. Double-click the transition you want to change.

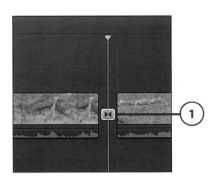

2. Drag a different transition from the list on top of the existing transition to change it.

Use the Precision Editor

If you want to make more granular changes to the transition, such as how long it lasts and where exactly the transition happens, you need to use the Precision Editor.

1. Right-click (or hold the Command key and click) the transition you want to change.

2. Select Show Precision Editor.

3. Drag the transition end markers to shorten or lengthen the duration of the transition.

4. Drag to move the transition to another point along the clip.

5. Touch to close the Precision Editor and save your changes.

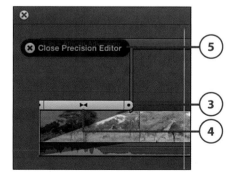

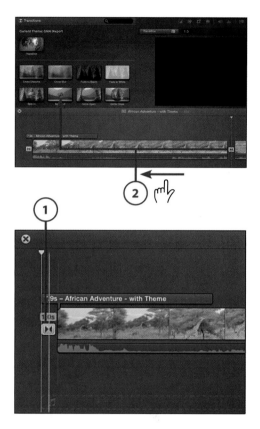

Removing a Theme

If you decide that you want to remove a video theme and gain complete control of your project, follow these steps.

1. Click Settings.

2. Click the name of the current theme.

3. Click No Theme.

4. Click Change.

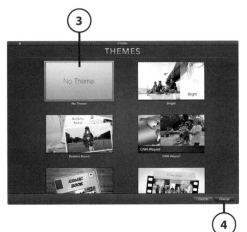

5. Click a transition to select it, and then press the Delete key to remove the transition.

6. Click Turn Off Automatic Content.

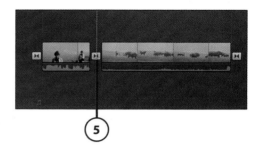

Choose a Trailer type

In this chapter, you find out how to create a movie-theater-style trailer for your video. Topics include the following:

→ Creating a trailer
→ Adjusting the trailer
→ Sharing the trailer

9

Creating and Customizing Trailers

A trailer is a short, fun, and well-put-together teaser for your video. You can send it to your friends or share it publically as a way to show your viewers what you are working on.

Creating a Trailer

When you create a new trailer, you can choose a style of trailer to use. The list of trailers you can choose from covers the typical trailer types you might see in the movie theater, such as adventure, documentary, action, and so on.

1. Click Create.

2. Click Trailer.

3. Scroll up and down to see all the templates. Each trailer template indicates how long the final trailer will be and how many cast members it will include.

4. Click a template to select it.

5. Click Create.

6. In the Name field, type the name of your movie as it will appear in the trailer.

7. In the Event field, select the event that your trailer must use for source video. This is typically the same event you use when creating your movie.

8. Click OK to create your new trailer using the trailer template you chose.

What Does the Trailer Template Do?

When you choose a trailer template, iMovie creates a trailer for your movie complete with music, titles, and graphics. It places dummy clips into the trailer that you will replace with clips from your own source video. The trailer has very high production values. The music is synchronized with the different clips in the trailer; the combination of the music, types of clips, graphics, and titles produces the correct mood for the trailer. As you see later in this chapter, all you need to do is insert the correct type of clips into the predetermined slots, and you end up with a very professional trailer for your movie.

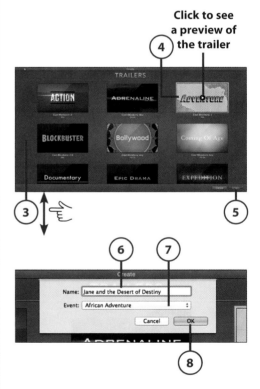

Click to see a preview of the trailer

Customize Your Trailer

After you choose the trailer template, you need to add your own clips to the trailer and enter the correct information for the credits screen.

1. Click the Outline tab.

2. Edit the name of your movie and its release date.

3. Edit the names of the cast member(s) and choose whether they are male or female.

4. Edit the name of your movie studio and choose the type of imagery you want shown when your studio name appears.

5. Scroll down for more outline choices.

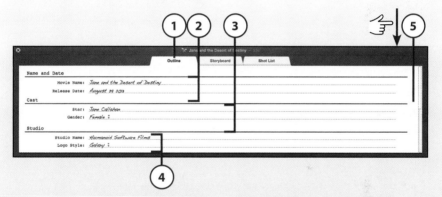

6. Edit the names to use in the credits.

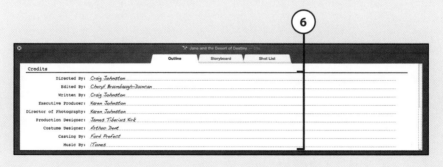

What Is a Storyboard?

A storyboard is a shot-by-shot layout of a movie. In the case of your trailer, it is a shot-by-shot layout of your trailer. As you scroll from top to bottom of the storyboard, you see how the trailer will be laid out from beginning to end. As you look at the storyboard, it is shown with the text that will be used and the types of video clips it wants to use. For example, the storyboard shows a dummy (or placeholder) clip, and the type of clip that should be used is written below it, such as Landscape, Wide, or Medium, and the name of your cast member(s). The dummy or placeholder clips visually indicate when you need to place a clip of one of the cast members, what they should be doing in the clip, or if you need scenery clips. All you need to do is find the right kinds of clips to use in each placeholder, and your trailer will take shape. If you don't like the predetermined text that is used in the cutaway scenes, you can change it.

7. Click the Storyboard tab.

8. Click the video clip placeholder you want to replace, unless iMovie has automatically selected it for you.

9. Click a portion of an existing clip you want to insert. The clip selection box is already the correct size for the length of the clip needed.

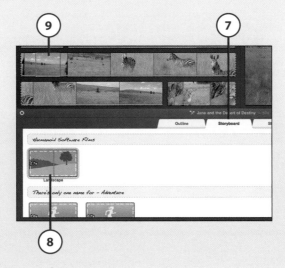

10. Repeat steps 8 and 9 until you have replaced all placeholder clips with clips from your video.

11. Click the text that iMovie has chosen for each cutaway scene, and replace it with your own text if you want to.

**What the text will
look like**

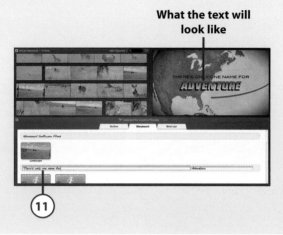

Ⓐ

Tweak the Clips

**Click to mute
the sound in
the clip**

After you have added your own clips to the placeholders, you might want to fine-tune exactly what part of the clip you want to use.

1. Click to change what portion of your clip to use.

2. Move the crop box left and right along the clip by moving your mouse left and right.

3. Click a portion of your clip to select it.

4. Click the X to save your changes.

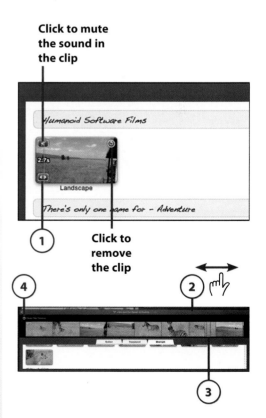

**Click to
remove
the clip**

Work with the Shot List

The Shot List tab shows all of your shots sorted by shot type, for example, all shots of your cast member(s), action shots, and so on. This view helps you eliminate any duplicate shots.

1. Click the Shot List tab.

2. Scroll through the categorized list of shots and make sure that all shots meet with your approval.

3. Click a shot to replace it with a different clip from your video.

4. Click a new clip in your video.

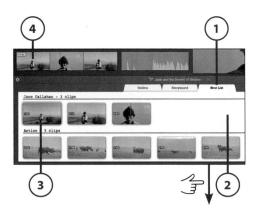

Adjusting Your Trailer's Look

When your trailer is almost ready, you can still adjust how it looks using the Adjust menu. As described in Chapter 7, "Editing Video Color, Brightness, and More," you can make adjustments to the clips used in your trailer. Note that you can only adjust your clips, not the predefined trailer objects like the cut scene text and colors or the music.

Have Even More Control Over Your Trailer

You might want to add to or edit how the trailer looks without the constraints of the trailer template. You can do this by converting your trailer to a movie. Beware that once your trailer has been converted to a movie, you cannot convert it back to a trailer. It is advisable to first make a copy of your trailer, and then convert the copy to a movie just in case you change your mind later. After your trailer has been converted to a movie, you will be able to edit every aspect of it as you would any movie, including the look and feel of transitions. You can even make the trailer longer or shorter by adding or removing clips. To convert your trailer into a movie, select File, Convert Trailer to Movie.

Sharing Your Trailer

When your trailer is ready, you can share it with friends, family, or publically using different online services like YouTube, Facebook, or Vimeo, or you can save it locally to your Mac.

1. Click the Share icon.

2. Click one of the methods for sharing.

The various methods for sharing a trailer from iMovie work the same as for sharing a movie. (The actual steps are covered in Chapter 10.) Each method starts back at this menu by clicking the relevant sharing option, such as Email.

Choose how to share your movie

In this chapter, you find out how to share your movie or trailer with others. Topics include the following:

→ Sharing your movie via email
→ Sharing your movie to online services
→ Exporting your movie to your hard disk

10

Sharing Your Movies

After you have created your movie, you might want to share it online or with a few select people via email.

Sharing Your Movie

When your movie is ready, you can share it with friends, family, or the general public.

1. Click the Share icon.

2. Click one of the methods for sharing.

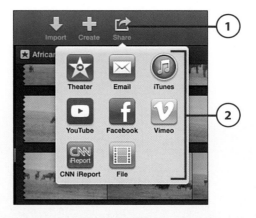

What Are Tags?

Tags are essentially keywords included with your trailer that allow you to search for it on your computer more easily; but more importantly, tags enable people on the Internet to find your trailer using these tags or keywords.

Share via Email

1. Click the title text to edit the title if you want to change it.

2. Click the Description text to edit the description if you want to change it.

3. Click the Tags text to edit or add more tags.

4. Click the Size field to select the size of the video. The larger the size, the more disk space the video requires.

5. Click the Share button to select the recipients of the email and send it.

What Does the Warning Mean?

When you share your movie via email, iMovie warns you if the amount of space that the movie will require is greater than 10 megabytes (MB). This is because most email providers artificially limit the size of incoming email attachments to 10MB. To reduce the amount of space the movie will require, reduce the size of the movie as described in step 4.

Share to iTunes

When you select the iTunes sharing option, you put your movie into iTunes, which means you can then synchronize or watch it on many different devices (such as Apple TV, iPods, iPhones, and iPads).

1. Click the title text to edit the title if you want to change it.

2. Click the Description text to edit the description if you want to change it.

3. Click the Tags text to edit or add more tags.

4. Click the Size field to select the size of the video. The larger the size, the fewer older devices your movie will be able to be viewed on.

5. Hover your mouse cursor over the check mark information icon to see which devices your movie will be able to be played on.

6. Click the Share button to import your movie into iTunes.

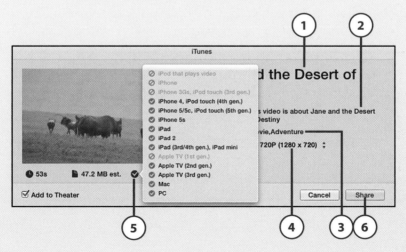

Share to YouTube

You need your own YouTube account before you can share your movie on YouTube.

1. Click the title text to edit the title if you want to change it.

2. Click the Description text to edit the description if you want to change it.

3. Click the Tags text to edit or add more tags.

4. Click the Size field to select the size of the video. It is normally best to always upload the largest size video to YouTube.

5. Click the Category field to choose the YouTube category for your movie.

6. Click the Viewable By field to choose who will be able to see your movie after you upload it to YouTube.

7. Click the Next button to enter your YouTube login and password and upload your movie to YouTube.

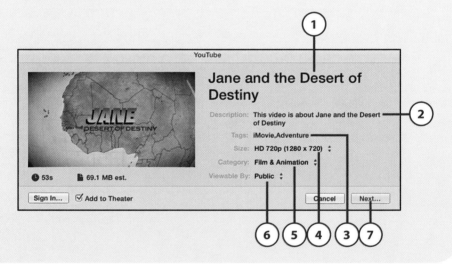

Share to Facebook

You need your own Facebook account before you can share your movie on Facebook.

1. Click the title text to edit the title if you want to change it.

2. Click the Description text to edit the description if you want to change it.

3. Click the Tags text to edit or add more tags.

4. Click the Size field to select the size of the video.

5. Click the Viewable By field to choose who will be able to see your movie after you upload it to Facebook.

6. Click the Next button to enter your Facebook login and password and upload your movie to your wall on Facebook.

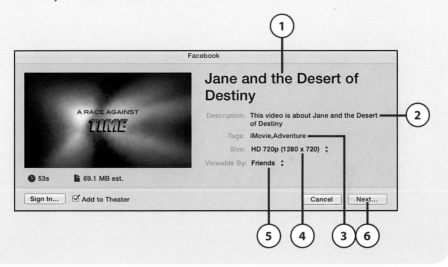

Share to Vimeo

You need your own Vimeo account before you can share your movie on Vimeo.

1. Click the title text to edit the title if you want to change it.

2. Click the Description text to edit the description if you want to change it.

3. Click the Tags text to edit or add more tags.

4. Click the Size field to select the size of the video.

5. Click the Viewable By field to choose who will be able to see your movie after you upload it to Vimeo.

6. Click the Next button to enter your Vimeo login and password and upload your movie to Vimeo.

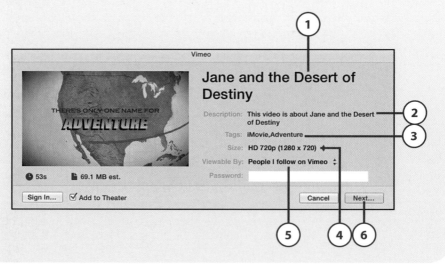

Share to CNN iReport

You need your own CNN iReport account before you can share your movie on CNN iReport.

1. Click the title text to edit the title if you want to change it.

2. Click the Description text to edit the description if you want to change it.

3. Click the Tags text to edit or add more tags.

4. Click the Size field to select the size of the video.

5. Click the Next button to enter your CNN iReport login and password and upload your
   movie to the CNN iReport website.

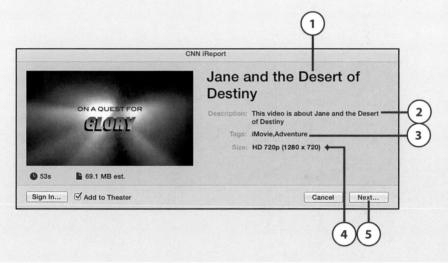

Save Your Movie to Your Mac Hard Disk

With this option, you can save your movie in QuickTime format as a file on your Mac's hard disk.

1. Click the title text to edit the title if you want to change it.

2. Click the Description text to edit the description if you want to change it.

3. Click the Tags text to edit or add more tags.

4. Click the Size field to select the size of the video.

5. Click the Next button to choose a folder where you want to save your movie.

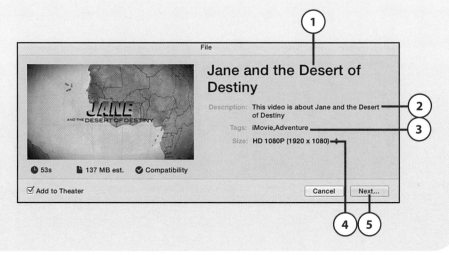

Seeing Where Your Movie Is Shared

If you need to see where you have shared your movie, follow these steps.

1. Click your movie to select it.

2. Select Window, Movie Properties.

3. Click the Shared icon to view where your movie has been shared.

4. Click the arrow to be taken to your movie that has been shared to an online service like YouTube, Vimeo, or Facebook.

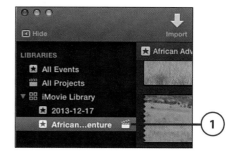

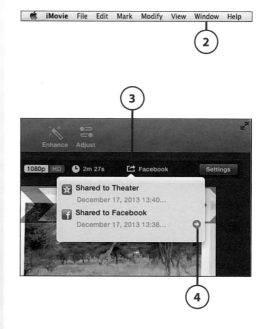

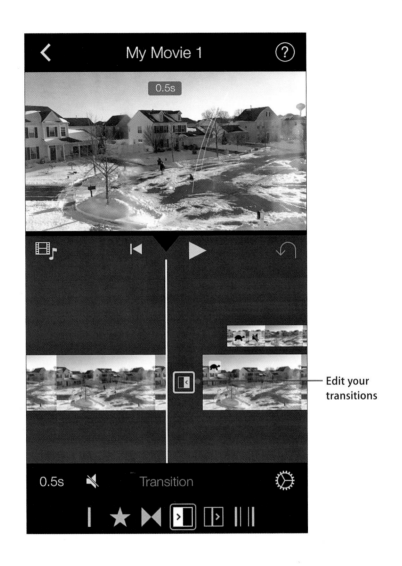

Edit your transitions

In this chapter, you see how to use iMovie on your iPhone and iPad. Topics include the following:

→ Creating a new project
→ Adding video
→ Adding a voiceover
→ Creating a trailer
→ Using transitions

Using iMovie on Your iPhone and iPad

Although you might not think of your iPhone or iPad as a place to put together videos, iMovie works extremely well on those devices. This chapter covers some of the main features of iMovie for iPhone and iPad. The figures are from an iPhone, but the same steps work on an iPad and iPod touch. Some icons on the iPad are in different parts of the screen, but the steps are the same.

Creating a New Movie Project

When creating a new movie project, you have to choose a theme.

1. Touch Projects.
2. Touch the New Project icon.
3. Touch Movie.

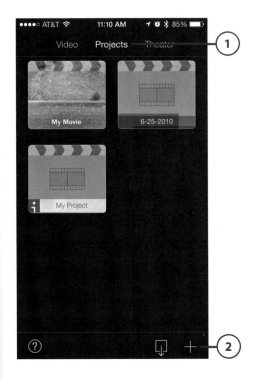

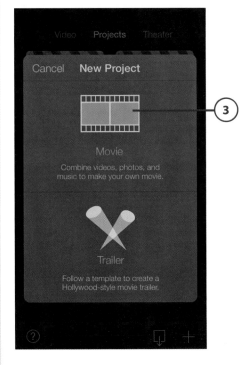

4. Touch a movie theme to select it.

5. Touch Create Movie.

4 **Touch to see a preview of the theme**

What Does the Theme Do?

When you choose a theme, iMovie pulls together clip transitions, opening and closing titles, and other titles that fit a style for the chosen theme. While you are creating your movie, you can add these elements to your movie at any time, or even choose a different theme. Unlike iMovie on the Mac, which automatically inserts all titles and transitions, iMovie on the iPhone and iPad leaves that up to you.

How Do I Name My Project?

Unlike iMovie on the Mac, which lets you name your project at creation time, iMovie on the iPhone and iPad uses an automatically generated name for your project at creation time. After you have added at least one movie clip to your project, you will be able to rename the project. To do this, on the screen that shows a list of your projects, touch the project that you want to rename. On the next screen, touch the project name that appears below the preview of your project and type a new project name.

The Movie Project Main Screen

After you create a new movie project, you are presented with the main iMovie movie creation screen.

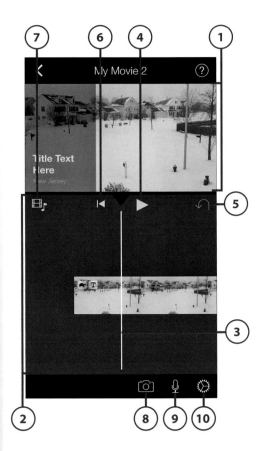

1. The preview window displays what is at the playhead and enables you to edit certain elements.

2. The timeline shows your movie's timeline along with titles, transitions, and speed indicators.

3. The video playhead indicates which frame is being displayed in the preview window.

4. Touch the Play icon to play your movie starting at the location indicated by the playhead.

5. Touch the Undo icon to undo the most recent change you made to your movie. Touch and hold to redo your most recent change.

6. Touch to jump to the beginning of the clip that is currently under the playhead. Touch repeatedly to get back to the beginning of your movie's timeline.

7. Touch the Media Import icon to add video, audio, or pictures to your movie's timeline.

8. Touch the Camera icon to record video or take a picture and immediately add it to your movie's timeline.

9. Touch the Microphone icon to record a voiceover track for your movie, starting at the position of the playhead.

10. Touch the Settings icon to change the settings for your movie project, including the theme, whether you want the theme music to be used, if you want the pitch of the audio to change when you adjust the speed of a movie clip, and if you want to add a fade-in from black or fade-out to black effect.

Adding Video, Photos, and Audio

Probably the first thing you want to add to your project is some multimedia.

1. Touch the Media Import icon.

2. Touch Video to see your available video.

3. Touch Photos to see your available photos.

4. Touch Audio to see your available audio, which includes music you have on your iPhone or iPad, audio you have recorded, and iMovie's built-in sound effects.

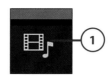

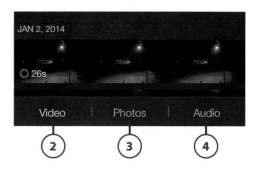

Add Video

When you add video, you are able to choose video that you have previously recorded on your iPhone or iPad, video that you have downloaded from the Internet, or video that you have synchronized from your computer using iTunes.

1. Touch the clip you want to add.

2. Drag the yellow markers left or right to select only the part of the clip you want to add to your project.

3. Touch Play to see a preview of the selected video.

4. Touch the Add icon to add the video to your project. The clip is placed into your project at the position of the playhead.

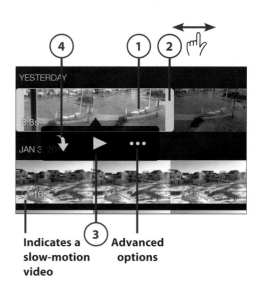

Indicates a slow-motion video

Advanced options

>>>Go Further

ADDING VIDEO AS PICTURE IN PICTURE AND OTHER OPTIONS

If you touch the Advanced Options icon, you are presented with advanced methods of adding the video clip. You can choose to only add the audio from the selected clip to your project, or add the selected clip as a cutaway clip, which means that during playback the main video cuts away to the cutaway clip. You can also add the clip as a Picture in Picture clip, which means that during playback the selected clip plays in a small window overlayed on the main clip. Finally, you can add the clip as a Split Screen clip, which means that the screen is split into two parts and the selected clip plays in the second part of the screen.

Add the clip as a cutaway   **Add the clip as a split screen**

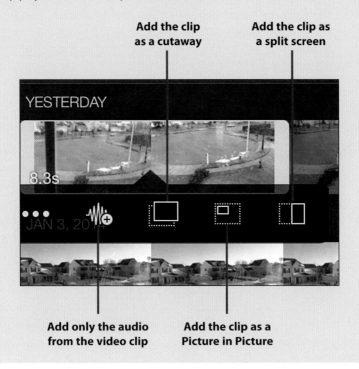

YESTERDAY

8.3s

JAN 3, 20

Add only the audio from the video clip   **Add the clip as a Picture in Picture**

Add Photos

You can add photos from any photo album on your iPhone or iPad.

1. Touch an album to see the photos in it. This example uses the Camera Roll.

2. Touch a photo to add it to your project at the position of the playhead.

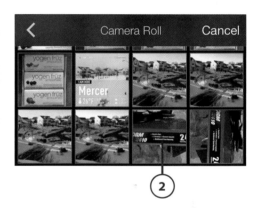

Add Audio

You can add audio from music you have purchased in iTunes, music you have downloaded through other sites, and iMovie built-in theme music and sound effects.

1. Touch to select either iMovie Theme Music or Sound Effects. If you want to select music that you own, touch Albums, Artists, or Songs; touch Playlists to select music that you have in a playlist. In this example, we add a song.

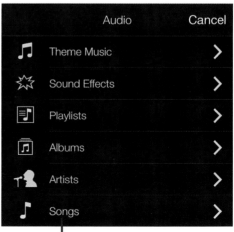

2. Touch a song to select it.

3. Touch Play to preview the song.

4. Touch the Add icon to add the song to your project.

Why Are Some Songs Unavailable?

If you try to add music you have purchased in iTunes, iMovie shows you all of the music that you own, even songs that aren't loaded onto your iPhone or iPad. If a song is grayed out, or starts with (Unavailable), it means that that song is not synced to your iPhone or iPad. Open the Music app, find the song, and touch the iCloud icon to download it to your device. If it still shows as unavailable in iMovie after you have downloaded it, then the song is protected by DRM and cannot be used in your movie project.

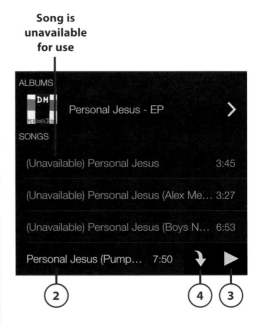

Song is unavailable for use

Touch to download the song to your iPhone or iPad

Editing Your Project

After you have your video, photos, and audio added to your movie project's timeline, it's time to edit and fine-tune your movie.

Add Titles

You can add titles to the beginning, end, or anywhere along your project timeline. The look of the titles is determined by the theme you have selected.

1. Position your timeline so that the playhead is directly over the place where you want to add a title. In this example, we add an opening title at the start of the timeline.

2. Touch the clip to select it.

3. Touch Video (unless it is already highlighted).

4. Touch Title.

5. Touch the type of title you want. In this example, we use an Opening title.

6. Touch Title Text Here to type in your own title text.

7. Touch the Text icon to select the style of the title text, including title text that uses animation.

8. Touch the Location icon to add location information to the title text. If you use this option, iMovie adds your current location just below the title text.

9. Touch to mute or unmute the title text's animation sound effect (if it has one).

10. Touch outside of the clip to save your changes.

More on iMovie Location Text

iMovie can optionally include your location to the title text you add. Location information is only available for Opening titles. If you use this feature, touch the GPS location arrow to let iMovie use your current location, or use the Search feature to find place names. You can also manually edit the location once it has been chosen.

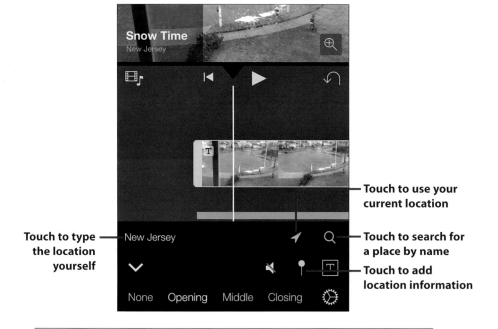

Touch to use your current location

Touch to type the location yourself

Touch to search for a place by name

Touch to add location information

Speed Up or Slow Down a Clip

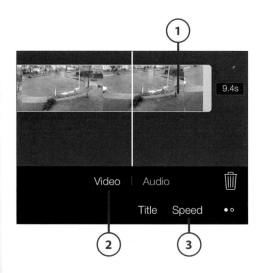

You can speed up or slow down the playing speed of a movie clip. For clips recorded in slow motion (slo-mo) on an iPhone 5S (and future iOS products), you can speed them up.

1. Touch the clip you want to change the speed for.

2. Touch Video (unless it is already highlighted).

3. Touch Speed.

4. Drag the Speed slider left or right to either slow down or speed up the clip.

5. Touch outside of the clip to save your changes.

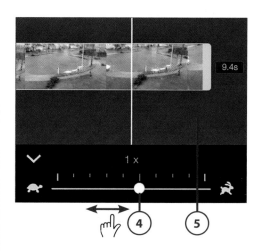

Slow Motion (Slo-Mo) Clips

Video that you originally recorded on your iPhone 5S in slow motion (also known as slo-mo) is recorded at 120 frames per second (fps). Regular video is recorded at 30fps. When you play slo-mo clips, they are effectively playing at one-fourth (¼) speed compared with regular clips, so when you bring up the Speed slider with a slo-mo clip selected, it shows that the speed is ¼. The difference between a clip recorded in slo-mo on an iPhone 5S and a regular clip recorded at 30fps that you are slowing down in iMovie is quality. If you slow down a clip recorded at 30fps to a ¼ speed, you are effectively playing it at about 7fps, so the video will appear a bit jerky. If you use a clip recorded in slo-mo on an iPhone 5S then at ¼ speed it is actually 30fps and at full speed it is 120fps.

Trim a Clip

You might want to trim the length of a clip in your timeline to make it shorter.

1. Touch the clip you want to trim.

2. Drag the yellow trim handle to shorten the clip.

3. Touch outside of the clip to save your changes.

The clip time should decrease

Zoom In

You might want to zoom in to a specific area on a clip.

1. Touch the clip you want to zoom.

2. Touch the Zoom icon.

3. Use your thumb and forefinger to zoom in and out of the clip. Spread your thumb and forefinger apart to zoom in, and pinch them back together to zoom out.

4. Touch outside of the clip to save your changes.

Duplicate a Clip

You might have a clip that you need to duplicate.

1. Touch the clip you want to duplicate.

2. Touch the More icon to see more options. If you are using an iPad, all the options are already on the screen.

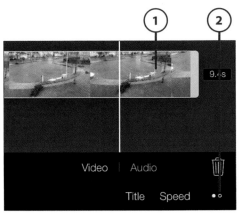

3. Touch Duplicate. A copy of the selected clip is made and placed in the timeline to the right of the original clip.

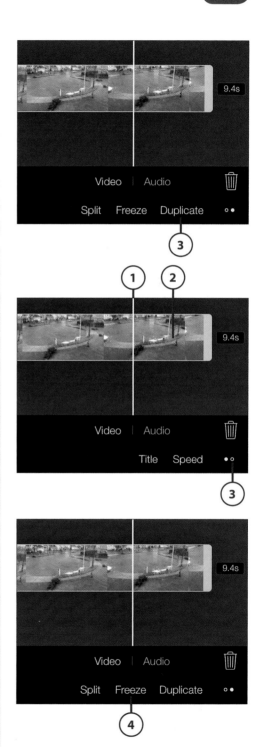

Create a Freeze Frame

When you create a freeze frame, iMovie takes the current frame and creates a two-second freeze frame.

1. Move the clip so that the play-head is over the frame you want to create a freeze frame from.

2. Touch the clip to select it.

3. Touch the More icon to see more options. If you are using an iPad, all the options are already on the screen.

4. Touch Freeze. A two-second freeze frame is made and placed in the timeline at the playhead.

Split a Clip

Splitting a clip can be very useful if you want to apply different titles or slow down or speed up just part of the original clip. By splitting the clip, you can apply those changes to just the newly split-off clip.

1. Move the clip so that the play-head is over the place where you want to make the split.

2. Touch the clip to select it.

3. Touch the More icon to see more options. If you are using an iPad, all the options are already on the screen.

4. Touch Split. The original clip is split into two clips at the play-head.

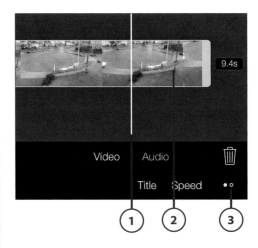

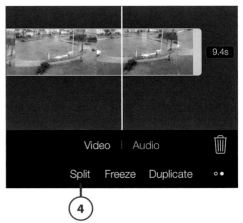

SPLITTING WITH A SWIPE

You can split a clip quickly by swiping down over the playhead. To do this, move the timeline so that the playhead is directly over the point where you want to split the clip. Touch the clip to select it. Swipe down directly over the playhead, and your clip will be sliced into two clips. It takes a bit of practice, but when you master the technique, it will save you time.

Delete a Clip

1. Touch the clip you want to delete.

2. Touch the Delete icon.

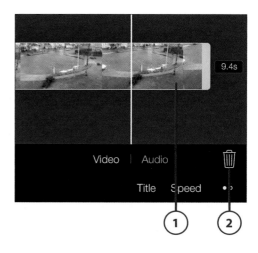

Change the Clip Volume

1. Touch the clip you want to change the volume for.

2. Touch Audio.

3. Drag the Volume slider to increase or decrease the volume of the clip.

4. Touch outside of the clip to save your changes.

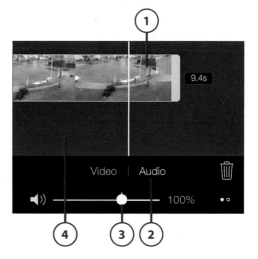

>>>Go Further

EDITING A PICTURE IN PICTURE

When you add a clip to be a Picture in Picture, notice that it appears above the clip it will be inserted into. You can change the position of the Picture in Picture and make it larger or smaller. To do this, touch the Picture in Picture clip to select it. Touch the + icon and use your thumb and forefinger to do the pinch-to-zoom gesture inside the Picture in Picture image to make it larger or smaller. Touch the Move icon and then drag the Picture in Picture to a new position.

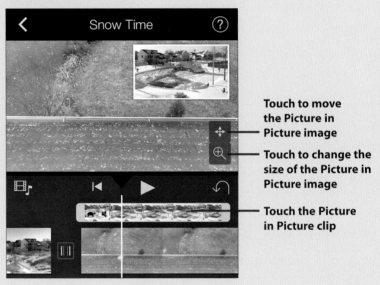

Touch to move the Picture in Picture image

Touch to change the size of the Picture in Picture image

Touch the Picture in Picture clip

Detach the Audio from a Clip

1. Touch the clip you want to detach the audio from.

2. Touch Audio.

3. Touch the More icon for more options. If you are using an iPad, all the options are already on the screen.

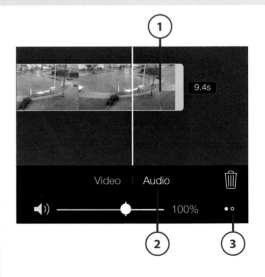

4. Touch Detach. The audio from the clip appears as a separate clip below the video clip.

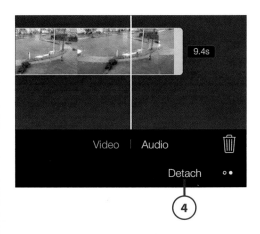

Why Detach Audio?

Detaching the audio from your video clip allows you to edit just the audio. This allows you to treat the audio track as its own clip. You can split the audio clip, delete parts of the audio clip, speed it up, slow it down, duplicate it, and so on.

Audio Tracks

Audio tracks are shown in the timeline using colors to indicate what kind of audio it is. If an audio track is blue or purple, it means that it is foreground audio. If an audio track is green, it means that it is the background audio. You can only have one background audio track, but many foreground tracks. Background audio is typically a music track, but not necessarily. Background audio is always softer than the foreground audio. At any time, you can switch an audio track to be the background audio, or make the background audio into a foreground audio track. Finally, you can make any audio track fade in or fade out.

Fade Audio

Audio tracks (including audio that you may have detached from its original video clip) can be set to fade in and/or fade out.

1. Touch the audio clip you want to either fade in or fade out.

2. Touch the More icon for more options. If you are using an iPad, all the options are already on the screen.

3. Touch Fade.

4. Drag the yellow arrow to set how long the fade-in or fade-out takes.

5. Touch outside of the clip to save your changes.

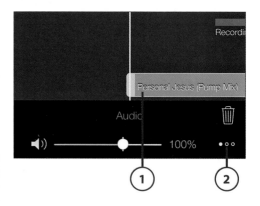

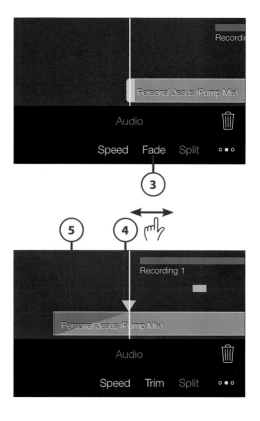

Switch Audio Between Foreground and Background

You can switch a background audio track to a foreground track or vice versa. In this example, we switch the background audio to the foreground.

1. Touch the audio clip you want to switch.

2. Touch the More icon twice (or once if you are using an iPad).

3. Touch Foreground.

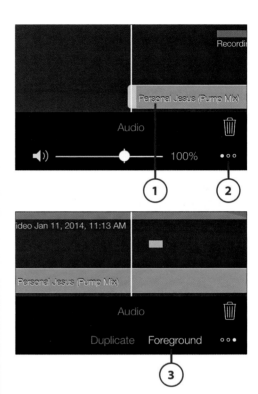

Record a Voiceover

Using your iPhone or iPad, you can record a voiceover track where you can narrate what is being seen, for example.

1. Drag the timeline so that the play-head is directly over where you want to start your voiceover.

2. Touch the Microphone icon.

3. Touch Record.

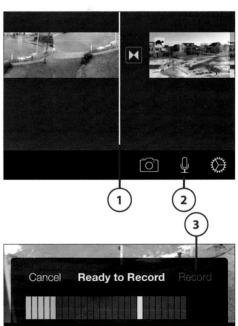

4. Wait for the countdown.

5. Start speaking.

6. Touch Stop when you are finished.

7. Touch Accept.

Edit a Transition

A transition is an effect that is used between two clips in your timeline. Based on the theme you choose, iMovie automatically inserts transitions. However, you might want to change which ones iMovie has used or edit them.

1. Touch the transition you want to edit.

2. Touch to change the duration of the transition.

3. Touch the Speaker icon to mute or unmute the transition's sound effect (if it has one).

4. Choose a different type of transition.

5. Touch outside of the transition to save your changes.

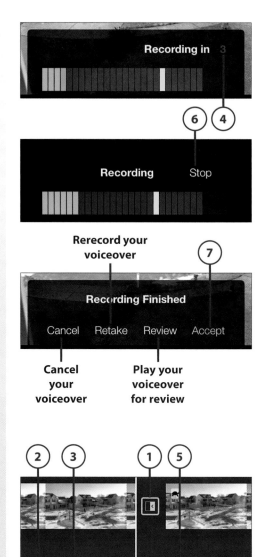

Recording in 3

6 4

Recording   Stop

Rerecord your voiceover

7

Recording Finished

Cancel   Retake   Review   Accept

Cancel your voiceover

Play your voiceover for review

2   3   1   5

0.5s   Transition

4

Can I Create a Trailer?

Just like iMovie on the Mac, you can create a very professional looking trailer for your movie. The steps for creating a trailer and the screens used are the same as iMovie on the Mac; read Chapter 9, "Creating and Customizing Trailers," for more information.

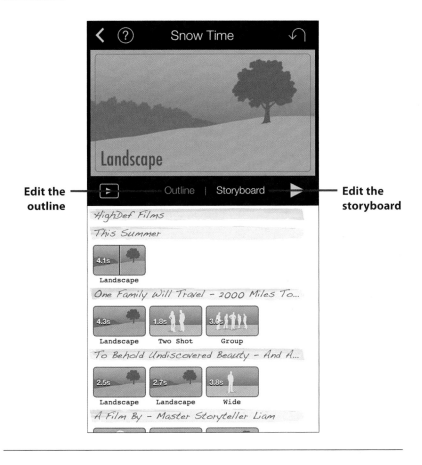

Edit the outline — (left label)

Edit the storyboard — (right label)

Sharing Your Movie or Trailer

After your movie or trailer is finished, you can share it with friends and family using email, text message, AirDrop or video sharing sites, or social media.

1. Touch the trailer or movie you want to share. In this example, we share a movie.

2. Touch the Share icon.

Trailer   (**1**) **Movie**

**Touch to make
more edits**

(**2**)   **Touch the
name to
change it**

3. Touch the recipient's profile photo to send your movie or trailer to someone via AirDrop.

4. Touch the iMovie Theater icon to save your movie or trailer in your iMovie Theater.

5. Touch the Facebook icon to share your movie or trailer on Facebook.

6. Touch the YouTube icon to share your movie or trailer on YouTube.

7. Touch the Vimeo icon to share your movie or trailer on Vimeo.

8. Swipe right to see more choices.

9. Touch the CNN iReport icon to save your movie or trailer with CNN using CNN iReport.

10. Touch the Message icon to share your movie or trailer via text message.

11. Touch the Mail icon to share your movie or trailer via email.

12. Touch the Save Video icon to save your movie or trailer to your iPhone or iPad's camera roll, which will enable you to share it later using any service not listed here.

13. Touch the iTunes icon to save your movie or trailer to iTunes.

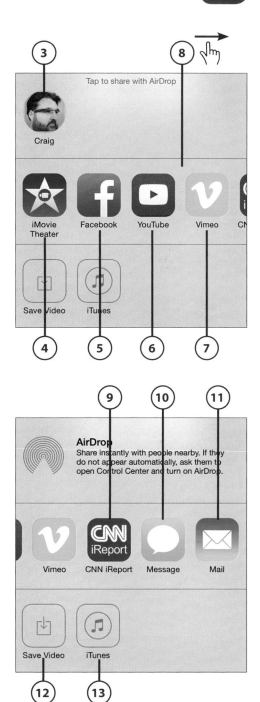

Index

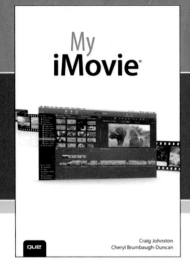

FREE Online Edition

Your purchase of *My iMovie*® includes access to a free online edition for 45 days through the **Safari Books Online** subscription service. Nearly every Que book is available online through **Safari Books Online**, along with thousands of books and videos from publishers such as Addison-Wesley Professional, Cisco Press, Exam Cram, IBM Press, O'Reilly Media, Prentice Hall, Sams, and VMware Press.

Safari Books Online is a digital library providing searchable, on-demand access to thousands of technology, digital media, and professional development books and videos from leading publishers. With one monthly or yearly subscription price, you get unlimited access to learning tools and information on topics including mobile app and software development, tips and tricks on using your favorite gadgets, networking, project management, graphic design, and much more.

Activate your FREE Online Edition at
informit.com/safarifree

STEP 1: Enter the coupon code: OZPEGDB.

STEP 2: New Safari users, complete the brief registration form. Safari subscribers, just log in.

If you have difficulty registering on Safari or accessing the online edition, please e-mail customer-service@safaribooksonline.com